Michel Stermann

My Maman Grète

*An educator from Germany
for orphans of Holocaust victims in France
and other family portraits*

Passport photograph, 1947

Michel STERMANN

My Maman Grète

An educator from Germany for orphans of Holocaust victims in France and other family portraits

TWENTYSIX – The self-publishing publisher

A Co-operation between the Random House Publishing Group and BoD – Books on Demand

© 2018 Michel Stermann

Manufacturing and publishing:

BoD – Books on Demand, Norderstedt, Germany

ISBN: 9783740744007

To Danielle and Fabien,
my dearest ones.

Preface to the reader of the English edition

This is not a professional translation of the French original but an English adaption by the author himself.

My 'mother language' is German whereas my 'father and school language' is French. Therefore, my English, learned later and taught as a foreign language at school, cannot be as rich and accurate. In short, I am not an English writer. However, I wanted to try and produce the English edition myself because the matter of this book intermingles so much of German and French that who else could have been a good translator for it?

This said, I apologize for the sometimes poor, clumsy, even wrong words and phrases I might use. I strongly hope that the reader's interest, pleasure and emotion will not be impacted excessively.

I also apologize to the British reader for using US-American spelling. I made this choice because I expected more American readers, starting with my American relatives and friends. With same hope as above.

To Maman Grète

Grète with Micha *in Le Raincy in November 1951*

Nobody was as present in my life as you, *Maman Grète*;[1] I missed nobody as much as you. Why did you leave me so early? You abandoned me twice. First by taking sleeping pills on March 22, 1953, when I was but one year, four

---

1 *Italics* are used in this book for words and expressions reproduced in their original languages, as well as for pseudonyms and nicknames. *Maman* is the French form of *Mommy*. *Grète* is the spelling of her first name used by my mother herself when she was living in France.

months and two weeks old. Deliberate action, irrational act, or Freudian slip? No one knows; I shall not know.

Second, without you being accountable for it, by and by, in the underground, you disappeared from conversations, evocations and pictures to look at.

I cannot bring you back physically, alas! But my desire is to erase the unspoken law of silence that weighed on me like a lead helmet. I want to call out your name to the whole world, *Maman Grète*! You have no grave anymore. Then this book shall be a monument to you.

Why do I call you *Maman Grète*? Because *Papa*, *Rémy*, married again two years later and there then also was a *Maman Magali*. As a matter of fact, my sister *Catia* and I used to speak for a while of *Maman Grète* and of *Maman Magali*. At that time for us still existed both the Margaret from Germany and the Margaret from Provence.[2]

Afterwards, speaking of the former, looking at her photo albums was discontinued, and the latter simply became *Maman*, voluntarily or not. Particularly after Gilles, our half-brother, was born, who had but one *Maman*. Later on, she became *Mam*, then *la Mère* (the Mother) and eventually just *Magali*.

My whole childhood was a blend of knowing and silence. As a young widower, *Rémy* was temporarily discharged from your children's care by your parents in Hamburg. They were the only grandparents I have known, because *Rémy*'s

---

[2] In German, *Grete* is a short form of *Margarete*. Some sources define *Magali* as a Provence dialectal variant for *Marguerite*; others rather from *Magdalena*; in the latter case, my sentence is not right anymore.

parents perished in the Camps. As far as I can remember, they too did not speak of you to me. To have the offsprings of their own flesh and blood before their eyes without feeling allowed to speak of you, whom they had cherished so much, what a pain for them also!

Then I said to myself, in my little child's head, that this is how it goes: 'once people are dead, one should not speak of them anymore, it is unmannerly. The grief for the survivors is too unbearable, one should not let them suffer, that is nasty.' Above all, I was thinking of *Papa* who, after having suffered a thousand martyrdoms in the so-called 'Concentration' Camps (what an understatement!), having lost there his father, mother, brother, uncles, aunts, cousins and others, furthermore had to endure your passing away, *Maman Grète*. I was to protect him, to keep at least him. Therefore I did not feel permitted to mention what burned my tongue.

My only conversations about the subject were with *Catia*, my elder sister. She would speak with a mysterious facial expression of these sleeping pills of which nobody knew whether or not you had taken too many intentionally when you were feeling too miserably. Of that falling out of the window that might have happened to you previously, perhaps while cleaning windows. Of that plaster corset that you seemed to have had to wear afterwards. But with adults… nothing anymore.

Room had to be made for the re-composed family, in that the first one, your family, had to withdraw by being 'swept under the carpet,' in spite of the connection with your parents, our grandparents, being preserved. What a paradox! Up to Gilles, whom they generously treated like another grandson, without any discrimination. He will have to suffer from this situation, by the way.

Since then, I bear all this within myself, still now as a retired man, one prostate cancer later.

You were the *Maman Grète* of whom I was not to speak and therefore, in a certain way, a shame, a stain on my history. You have not deserved such a fame, neither have I deserved this diffuse feeling of guilt. In fear of another severe disease, I have taken again a psychotherapeutic support to get some help, so that all these things might clear up and calm down. One conviction came out of it: I had to loudly proclaim your virtues, your nature, your history.

To help me for these tasks, I am not without tools. First, Genealogy; Danielle, my wife and life companion, had started previously a comprehensive and exciting research on her family, in which I am taking an active part. When I felt that my father was going downhill, and when he told me some particulars about his relatives, I felt as early as in 1999 the desire to pick up the torch of memory. I was certain now that it was my turn to deal with the history of our family. In wide portions, it is your story, *Maman Grète*, and the one of your relatives.

Second, as sole heir of your brother, my dear Uncle *Jacki*, I came in 2007 into possession of the house your parents had built. And, because they never disposed of anything, I found in it treasures of memories: photograph albums and negatives, your school notebooks, your diary as a teenager, the diaries your mother kept from 1917 to 1943, as well as the complete family letter exchange, including your letters from France to your parents and *Jacki*, from 1947 to March

1953.

Your letters tell a lot about your personality, your intelligence, your culture, your manual and artistic capabilities, your commitment, your sincerity, your care for others—especially for children—, your humor and your joyfulness. They do not tell much about your moments of discouragement which eventually will tear you of this life, because you do not want your dear ones remaining in Hamburg to worry. However, as they are, they can be an invaluable source of knowledge about you, my own pre-history and the story of my beginnings.

Of course, these letters were written in German. Their style is very familiar to me. I almost could have written them myself (except that my script is not as regular and neat). No wonder since I had partly the same educators as you, having spent many months with your parents. The spirit of your family is also in me.

It was your choice to travel to France and share the life of *Rémy*, your great love, and to become an educator for orphaned children of Holocaust victims.

For some time, I have been in touch with some of them who knew you and can tell about you, which is very soothing for me because you left only good memories to them. On the insisting request of one of them I started to translate from German to French your 150 letters from France.

Translating is different from just reading and making an inventory. Your spirit and your feelings penetrate much more into me. This is where I shall take most of the material out of which this book is made, as a complement to my research on our family tree and family history.

YOUR STORY

Your start in life

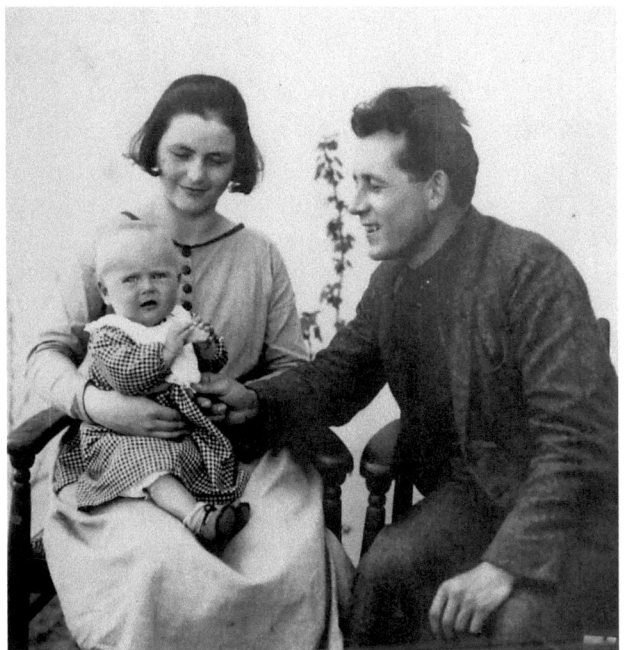

Grete and her parents

You come to this world as Grete[3] Meitmann, without a middle name, on Sunday, September 2, 1923 at 3:15 a.m. at the *Frauenklinik* (Women's Clinic) in Kiel.[4] Your parents were born in that town, as will be your brother *Jacki*, two

---

[3] *Grete* is the German spelling. For pronunciation reasons, her name was spelled *Grète* in France. I'll use the latter when appropriate, *i.e.* after her immigration in November 1947.

[4] See maps with the main locations mentioned, in the "Documents" Section at the end of this book.

years later. Your parents, although descending from Lutheran Protestants, were Socialists and no friends of priests. That is why you were not baptized upon your birth. But you were in the Nazi period, probably as a national-political obligation.

'Grete,' your first name, was not chosen without reason. This was the (shortened) name of your father's first great love, with whom he maintained a lively correspondence during World War I, while he was a combatant in the trenches. This other Grete renounced him shortly before he got his home leave from the army, causing him a great grief of love.

Is it not a little burdensome, even unconsciously, to be—so to speak—a compensation child for a lost love? These things are not easy to be seen through, however I cannot but keep thinking that the choice of your first name will play a part in your destiny.

On your civil registration birth record, based on a statement from the *Frauenklinik*, your father Karl Meitmann, aged thirty-two, is said to be a police auxiliary. He is in fact a civil commissioner with the mission of facilitating the transition of the Schleswig-Holstein Police from the Empire to the Republic.

Your mother, the beautiful Else Meitmann, née Adam, is then aged twenty-one, a trained furniture and home interior designer. After one year of marriage, you are their first child.

You reside in a western district of Kiel.

Kiel Hasseldieksdammer Weg 217 in 1925

From period photographs, I see that you live in a detached house where there is also a shop of the Consumer Cooperative. It has a garden where you can play in open air with *Jacki*, your brother, who will be born on March 12, 1925, and on this way discover Nature.

Your address is *Hasseldieksdammer Weg* 217 (Hasseldieksdamm Drive). This typical Northern-German dialectal name always would amuse your mother. You probably were provided with this residence by your maternal grandfather Hermann Adam, founder and manager of the Workers' Consumer Cooperative, after he had lost his job on a shipyard because he had been part of establishing a socialist-oriented worker union and organizing a strike.

Your other grandfather, Johannes Meitmann, had a similar story, by the way, but he died on the day before your parents' marriage. Too bad, you haven't known that one.

Neither have you your paternal grandmother; your father had lost his mother when he was seven; he was raised afterwards by a stepmother, as I was. Who said once that History does not repeat itself but keeps stuttering?

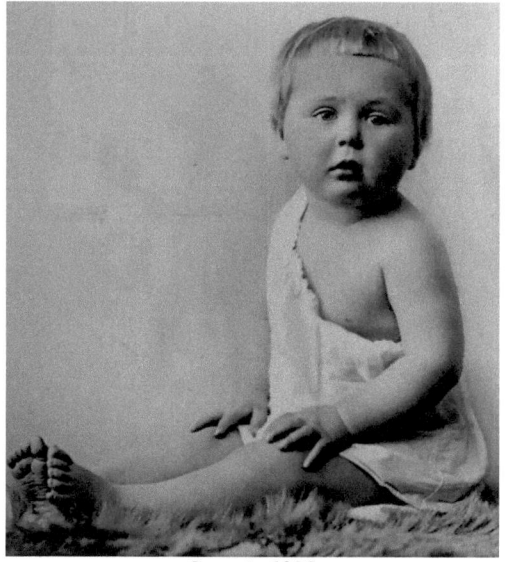
Grete in 1925

You are a sweet little child, pretty round face, with blond, stiff, square-cut hair, wide-open eyes, rather more grey than sky-blue, like your whole family, including my sister. Mine are not; they resemble the water in a glass in which several water-color brushes were rinsed: the color of all colors mixed.

Farewell from Kiel

In 1927, when you are about four, your family moves some sixty miles southwards to Altona. Later on, it will become a part of the 'Free and Hansa City' (city-state) of Hamburg, but at that moment this location still belongs to the State of Schleswig-Holstein, although it is within the urban area of Hamburg. Its name comes from the dialectal expression *'all to nah,'* meaning 'much-too-near.'

Your *Vati*[5] has been provided by his political party, the Social-Democratic SPD, with new responsibilities. He has established the *Reichsbanner Schwarz-Rot-Gold* for Schleswig-Holstein, a kind of paramilitary force that he leads, and he was elected as SPD District Secretary. He is more and more involved in his duties, so you now see him less often.

Simultaneously, you discover the large city of Hamburg, its maritime harbor, its subway and commuter trains, the Rathenaupark, which is more or less to replace your garden. Your address, by the way, is then *'Am Rathenaupark,'* showing that you are very close to this large and popular public garden.

Two years later, in 1929, a new commitment change for your father, new moving (you will know so many in your short life!). You leave Schleswig-Holstein for Hamburg-Fuhlsbüttel, a few miles to the northeast, known for its international airport and its prison.

---

[5] German form of *Daddy*, pronounced *'fahti.'*

You reside in a little apartment house built out of dark red bricks topped by a high tile roof with one upper story and roof apartments, located at *Maienweg* 231.

Fuhlsbüttel, Maienweg 231,in 2007

That house still is there in the twenty-first century, the last one at the corner of the street to the indirectly visible prison, surrounded with a garden in which *Jacki* and you again will be able to tire yourselves out, even with little playing companions. Still today the architecture does not look old-fashioned; the pavement is tree-lined. A rather pleasant place.

Your father was promoted within the SPD; he was elected as Hamburg regional chairman, later as a member of the regional and civic Parliament, the *Bürgerschaft*. He is very busy; many appointments, speeches and public meetings are to be prepared and performed, leaflets and articles to be written, election campaigns follow one another, for the *Bürgerschaft*, the *Reichstag*, the President; social class fights are to be carried out, as well as political ones against that Hitler gang, which is becoming more and more dangerous.

Anni, Oma, *Grete,* Mutti *and* Jacki *in 1925*

On September 9, 1929, your *Opa Adam* passes away in Kiel. I can see you on photographs of 1925 in your grandparents' home, perched on Hermann's high leather armchair or on the lap of your grandmother Anna, née Feist. These two seem to have been fond of you. *Oma*,[6] by the way, will survive you by eight years and even I shall know her. Your *Opa*'s[7] death certainly caused you grief, to your *Mutti* too.

School excursion – Jacki is allowed to go with Grete and her classmates, 1930

A great event happens in April 1930: holding a giant paper cone[8] filled with candies and goodies, with a brand new satchel on your back, you enter the elementary school. In that period, the school year would begin after Easter in some parts of Germany.

On other pictures, I can see you in the school yard, in front of the brick building, boys and girls aligned in mixed pairs, departing for a school excursion. Surprisingly, your little brother was allowed to come along; you are holding his hand. The boys wear a mariner suit or leather shorts, the girls flat round caps or a bell-shaped hat; all have small

---

[6] German form of 'Granny'.
[7] German form of 'Grandpa'.
[8] A German tradition for children's comfort on their first school day; one can see all new pupils holding huge cones on their way to school.

shoulder bags or backpacks.

I keep your school notebooks, among which the ones with your first writing attempts. You learn the *Sütterlin* script, a standard German neat handwriting you will keep until the end of the Nazi period. You write with heed, regularly and well-rounded. In his correspondence, your little brother *Jacki*, for his part, will dare our usual Latin script as early as in 1940.

You are a quick learner and will become a good pupil, particularly gifted for foreign languages, singing, music, drawing and handicraft.

Jacki too will have his turn to enter a pupil career, shortly before the events that will overturn the life of your whole family, of Germany, later of Europe and of the whole world.

Banished

The disaster occurs in January 1933. Adolf Hitler and his brutal, ruthless gangsters win the *Reichstag* election with a relative majority, form a government with the goodwill of the president, the elderly Lord Marshal von Hindenburg, and everything crashes.

Since all other parties were forbidden, your father begins a secret opposition. He contributes to spreading underground papers, to semi-official meetings.

With the Communists, the Nazis are incredibly brutal and quick but they also will act against the Socialists. In Hamburg, your *Vati* is at their head. Therefore they particularly target him. He gets arrested three times during meetings, on March 24 for three days, on May 2 for a couple of weeks and finally on June 16.

This time he does not come back so quickly. The Fuhlsbüttel prison had been changed into a concentration camp for political opponents and is named *Kolafu* in the *Gestapo* jargon. There he is in custody, so close to you, his family, so inaccessible. What an anxiety for your *Mutti* and for her children!

Some photographs show you during the summer vacations in Kiel with uncles and aunts, with *Oma* but without *Vati*. You now have a short hairstyle with shorter hair than your curly-headed brother. You are at the beach, laughing, because you are children, but how burdensome, how threatening must the general mood be!

Since the beginning of the dictatorship, your *Mutti* has interrupted her diary. Nothing at all written between January and November 1933. That is why I lose your track for a while, after the summer. Did *Jacki* and you return to Hamburg and to school? The times are uncertain. What will become of you, now?

Late in October, the events will happen in a rush. After the conclusion of some developments I shall explain in detail further down when telling his own story, your *Vati* is released but with the stipulation that he leaves Hamburg within twenty-four hours and refrains from any political activity. At last! That passed close by you all. There have been so many who never came alive out of the claws of *Gestapo* and SS!

Only: your whole life is to be re-built. The Meitmann family needs a home, an income, schools, a minimum of safety. In the underground, a network of helpers is at work. After waiting for a few days at the home of friends—which I could not identify—in Niendorf by the Lübeck Bight, your parents give you children in charge to your *Oma* and they settle far away in a lost West-Prussian hamlet.

Early in November 1933, your *Mutti* resumes her diary, with her arrival in Schmagorei, in the middle of nowhere. In that far East, she wonders if she is somewhere "between *Mongolei* and *Mandschurei*." In fact, the place is located East of Frankfurt/Oder, in the *Kreis*[9] of West-Sternberg, between the communities of Drossen and Zielenzig. After the war, this area will become Polish and the place will be

---

[9] District, county.

named *Smogory*. Apart from the railroad station, its sole particularity is the lignite mine. That brown coal has been the traditional energy source in the eastern parts of Germany. With the complicity of a party mate who is a manager of the mining *kombinat*,[10] your *Vati* is employed in the mine office as a payroll accountant.

Schmagorei November 1933

As it seems, the mine provides a service accommodation in a cottage. Light-tinted plaster, steep tile gable roof with attic rooms, gable windows, small garden around, entrance through a small glazed veranda on top of a few steps. Electric power is provided, but cold, very cold water only outside from the manual pump with wooden casing. A single lignite oven is the sole means of heating and cooking. The surroundings consist of village margin and fields as far as the eye can reach. Mine, station and village school are

---

[10] Large industrial enterprise.

reachable by foot.

This village certainly reminds your *Mutti* of her parents' rural Lower-Silesian roots. In the past, she had paid visits to her uncles, aunts, and cousins in these also distant easterly but further southerly regions, a lengthy, adventurous railroad trip with poultry in the compartment and chamber pot for the children under their mother's protecting skirt.

In December, your *Oma* brings you too to Schmagorei, your little brother and yourself. There are also long railroad hours from Kiel via Hamburg, Berlin, and Frankfurt/Oder. Your grandmother stays over Christmas and New Year with you. She travels back later than planned because she sprained one of her ankles by falling on black ice.

For you as a city child, *Maman Grète*, it means discovering a rural environment: much nature, little comfort, many animals, a small school, peasant classmates.

It also is a time of reticence. Do not tell who you are, where you come from, what your father did before. In your father's employment record book is written under "Previous occupations of longer duration" plainly "representative." Anyway, in these times of general prudence, nobody seems to be too curious. You all have kept your true identities, but in this lost corner of Germany the authorities are not too persnickety. Only the mine manager is informed; he is friendly and among your protectors.

Nonetheless, the atmosphere is burdensome. You miss your books, your toys, your records, your accustomed domestic devices, and your furniture. Your *Vati* is gloomy. Politics was his whole life. He misses speeches, discussions, convincing others, managing, acting. He is like a lion in a cage. Trifles can make him furious.

A little ray of sunshine for you, as early as 1934. Your friend and protector from the *kombinat* management comes visiting, with, as a gift, a very young German shepherd dog; Tello will be his name.

Tello, Grete, and Jacki *1934 in Schmagorei. Notice the water pump.*

You shine; you have a special love for pets. I can see how you bathe him in a big metal tub close to your house; I also see him in other photographs, sometimes in a large wire-mesh cage. One year later I see you in company of a Fox Terrier, Axel. How strange ... do dogs not last long with your family, or is it someone else's dog?

Fortunately, you spend your 1935 summer vacation in Kiel, as evidenced by some photographs. Even your *Vati* is there with you. Only sixty miles from the location where he is forbidden to stay, is it not a little risky?

Summer 1935, Grete (arrow) with family and relatives onboard her uncles' fishing boat in Laboe

Anyhow, I see him with you on the wooden fishing boat belonging to his brothers and in the seaside resort Laboe by the Baltic near Kiel.

In fall 1935 the small village school in Schmagorei is not sufficient anymore. Your parents provide a more upscale educational institution in Drossen, the next location to the West. You commute daily by rail.

You spend the 1936 summer vacation in Lower Silesia, in the root farm of the Adam family in Putschlau near Glogau, still operated by one of *Mutti*'s aunts, and at the home of cousins in Polkwitz, a little further to the southwest. With a shining face, you are riding bareback a white draft horse fitted with a thick collar. The family archive shows that it was not a pure leisure trip. Like all Germans under the Nazi regime, each one of your parents must set up his own so-called *Ahnenpass*[11] with baptism and marriage certificates of his ancestors, to prove there are no Jews among them. Your mother seems to have taken a liking to it and she complements her research on the spot, of which I keep her notes.

A few years afterwards, you will draw a large family tree in which all persons are provided with their professional attributes. When you know their faces, you draw caricatures. You depict yourself with a beret on your head and carrying a violin case because you will receive serious music lessons. I keep your violin and its case as a precious relic together with the family archive. Strings and bow horsehair have disintegrated into dust.

I would use this instrument as a music toy during my vacations at your parents' home. When I asked *Mutti* whose violin it was, she told me it was hers so she did not have to mention you. Too bad! I would have been so proud of you. I only understood much later.

---

[11] Literally, 'ancestor passport.'

Drossen, in 1936

Drossen, in 1936, view from the balcony

In October 1936, the whole family moves to Drossen. Your *Vati* will now have to be the daily commuter by rail. You reside then in a large, apparently brand-new kind of mountain lodge with plastered ground floor, wooden upper floor with a balcony. It is large enough, as it seems, for two families. You are at the city margin; your wooden balcony overlooks a lake and a wide landscape; in the background, to the right, the little town around its church tower. You seem to be better equipped than in Schmagorei. In spite of it, you only stay shortly there since the next moving (again!) takes place as early as April 1937.

Back to a big city

Your *Vati*, still a payroll accountant, is transferred to the *kombinat* headquarters in Berlin.

Berlin, 1938, Grete is 15

You need a new home, an occasion occurs. Or maybe it was the other way around: the apartment opportunity motivating the job transfer. I do not know. A couple of your parents' youth friends, Frieda and Andreas Gayk, cede their rental agreement to them, if I understand correctly.

You live on the fifth floor, *Knesebeckstrasse* 16, in the so-called garden house (the back building), in Berlin-Charlottenburg, west of the city center; there is a small balcony with a view of some trees, on which the four of you will often be photographed.

After the war still to come, Andreas will become the very popular mayor who will push the reconstruction of Kiel, and the kind Frieda, a diabetic, will go blind. I knew and liked her in my childhood.

Well, back to a big city, the biggest, the capital. It is enchanting. Stores, subway, double-decker buses, parks, woods, lakes for water sports, etc. Much more social life, relatives, friends.

For your part, *Maman Grète*, you stay full-time in a school with advanced education methods for highly gifted, in Schöneiche, a castle outside Berlin to the East. You stay in permanent contact with your parents by means of simple, non-illustrated postcards which allow a limited text page each.

Your *Vati* will own a sailing boat, a second one later on. To move on water is his passion, which—by the way—he shall transmit to me, although I hardly fulfill it now.

Summer vacation, 1937, again in Kiel, with your two uncles' fishing boat, the seaside, and beach life. Now you are a handsome girl. And then life goes on, full-time school, sailing on weekends. You meet with your uncle Hans Adam and the Kiel friend families which also live in Berlin, Gayks, Brodersens...

What is this? In 1938 you are in a photograph, together with *Oma*, *Mutti*, and *Jacki* in front of the Brandenburg Gate. I see your grandmother also comes to visit you sometimes.

Brandenburg Gate, Berlin in 1938: Mutti, *Grete,* Oma *and* Jacki

Your parents' marriage keeps getting worse. Arguments, unconcealed mutual infidelity, considered but not performed separation because of financial obstacles, the political situation, and you children. The general atmosphere is stormy, tense: upcoming sounds of war.

In spite of this situation, the four of you undertake in July 1939 a big sailing tour on the chain of lakes, rivers and canals from Berlin to the North, as far as the *Müritzsee*, one of the largest lakes of that area. Photographs and an illustrated 'Logbook' bear witness of it. Big adventure and last enterprise in peacetime.

War

Then, the war bursts out. First British bombs fall on the capital as early as 1939, then on Hamburg and Kiel which will count among the most heavily destroyed cities. For more than five years you will have to live with the nerve-shaking howl of alarm sirens, nights in cellars, explosions, giant blazes, flak shots, victim and damage discoveries, catastrophic rumors going around, worrying for far-living relatives and friends, endless wait for life signs.

In her diaries, *Mutti* gives detailed reports about it. The family archive also contains the post card exchanges between Kiel and Berlin, with the dictator's medal profile on the stamps. Fortunately, the men in your family will not, unlike millions others, be grabbed and crushed by the Army: *Vati* is too old, *Jacki* is too young.

Grete and Jacki *in Berlin on the balcony at Knesebeckstrasse 16 in 1940*

You attend both final high school forms and pass the *Abitur*[12] on April 1, 1941. You are not yet seventeen, so you are in advance by two years.

At once, you have to do your half-year working duty. In the Nazi period, all youngsters of both genders must perform an unpaid mandatory duty. Your choice is to travel to your *Oma*'s in Kiel and become a house maid, mainly in charge of nursing two children, at the home of Dr. Hermann Andersen, a rich Kiel industrial who is head of a metal building company. At that time already, you felt attracted to educating children, as a little *Mutti* for them.

But there is war; because of the naval base and the shipyards, one bomb attack happens after the other. Eventually, the city area will be destroyed to over ninety percent. During a period of particularly intensive bombings, the Andersen family seeks some relief in their secondary home in Lübeck, a little offside, taking you with them.

You often enquire about *Oma*. On your days off you are with her. You have to descend to the air-raid shelter almost daily. For the whole duration of the war, your *Oma*'s homes will be bombed-out twice. Every time it happens she must seek a refuge at friends' or relatives'.

During your stay in Kiel, you maintain a vivid correspondence with your parents in Berlin. You send life signs, beg for some and receive them. You beg for sending your food tickets remaining in Berlin, exchanging tobacco tickets for other ones with your father.

---

[12] German high-school final examination, opening access to college. Usually taken at the age of 19.

Because the goods seized in countries occupied by the *Wehrmacht* are not meant primarily for the German civil population, but for Army, SS, *Gestapo*, and Party bosses, necessity reigns, and German civilians are forced to use food stamps just like the occupied populations. In Kiel, the situation is often even worse because bombs partly destroyed shops, warehouses and the feeder traffic. One should have in mind that the first victim of the Hitler regime was the German people.

Nevertheless, the postal service seems to have operated until 1945 and no shipment of the Meitmann family got lost. It also was by mail that your parents asked you the delicate question of your future, of resuming your education, of the career you aimed at.

Vati would like to see you in a teaching occupation, a secured official career. However, you cannot make a decision. On the one side you would not like to disappoint your father. On the other, you find the necessary studies too dry, the career too austere. Moreover, you would have been obliged to submit to the National-Socialist instruction; that is why the perspective of such a profession makes you feel rather nauseous.

Your ideal would be to use your talent for foreign languages for taking care of children in Britain or France, even though at that time it may look utopian. It is a real moral torture for you.

Psychic crisis and then seamstress apprenticeship

In October 1941, after achieving your labor service, you return to Berlin. Arguments with *Vati* about your future and—again and again—quarrels in your parents' marriage. *Jacki* acts as if he does not notice, but he suffers silently. Like a good girl, you obey and register at the *Friedrich-Wilhelm-Universität*, in German and Pedagogy.

But it has gone too far, exceeding the limits of your self-control. You do not know anymore what you want to do. After an attempt to be accepted in a theater school, you suffer from violent mood fluctuations.

On December 21, 1941, you are admitted to the University Neurologic Clinic of the *Charité* Hospital. Scenes of madness, of self-aggression, of complete despondency. The most advanced methods of the period are tried on you, including barbiturates, insulin, and electrical shocks.

Totally shaken, your *Mutti* often comes to visit you. You do not always accept seeing her; your *Vati* never. On February 4, 1942, you seem—at last—to have turned back to an apparently satisfied and obedient calmness.

The Meitmann family in Berlin on the balcony at Knesebeckstrasse 16 in 1940

For a few months you return to college. Late in September 1942, at end of half-year, you nonetheless completely abandon your studies and follow a totally different career. You make use of your manual skills by entering an apprenticeship in a theater costume-making company. It is named *Theaterkunst* and is located at *Schwedterstrasse* 9. Six weeks later, you start as an apprentice with the seamstress Hilde Romatzki, *Kurfürstendamm* 28.

New change on February 5, 1944: *Feldmarschall* Hermann Göring has decided to evacuate all dispensable civilians out of Berlin. Everyone has to take care of his own dwelling place. From now on your family is torn to pieces, till end of war.

Through, I think, your Hermberg friends and their Röhrdanz acquaintances, your parents find a home for you in Jena, *Wartburgstrasse* 6; lodger is Mrs. Anna Katharina Klingbeil. You resume your seamstress for lady garments apprenticeship in the 'Fashion House' *Modehaus Smyrek*,

Bachstrasse 3. You will achieve the professional certificate, with production of a 'masterpiece,' a very sophisticated dress.

The correspondence has not been interrupted: news, life signs. Your brother comes to your place in Jena; for health reasons and with a little luck and cheating, he has avoided an Army enrollment.

Peace

On one beautiful day in April 1945, you have a glimpse on soldiers wearing an unusual uniform: Americans. You are rid of the Hitler dictatorship, the end of war is near. You will see your *Vati* arriving on a bicycle. For days and days he rode and pressed the pedals, coming all the way from Berlin. He manages to hire a truck that brings you with all your stuff back to Hamburg.

Mutti is missing; you enquire by letter in Kiel and—oh, miracle!—there she is. On a bicycle, too, she had covered the nearly two hundred miles from the Oranienburg area where she lastly lived and worked. Sighs of relief! Once more achieved: Your family is reunited.

In Hamburg, your *Vati* will work for rebuilding a local SPD Organization. Because your home in Fuhlsbüttel now is occupied, you have temporarily been allocated the apartment of a Nazi-bigwig family that has been arrested or is on the flight, I do not know exactly. So, your new address is *Hallerstrasse* 25, for over one year. Your family's Berlin furniture is somewhere in a warehouse; your father will need to have it delivered by a consolidated transport company, which will take several months. It will arrive in a poor condition.

Willy-nilly, life will restart in a devastated Hamburg, where the most terrible need reigns. Everything is missing, the waiting lines get longer and longer, the winter will be awful.

According to your employment record book, you are, from July to October 1945, an employee of the 'fashion house' *Modehaus Horn*. The record does not tell us if you have applied your seamstress certificate or by necessity are working as a simple salesperson. Anyway, between October 1945 and late in February 1946, you are unemployed. For a skilled but beginning seamstress, there probably are few job opportunities. Is this the reason why you change your occupation, or did you do it by choice? My sources are mute on that subject: no diaries anymore, naturally no correspondence between family members and—of course—I was told nothing about that time.

Actually, you will apply your skills in foreign languages. All North-West Germany has become a British occupation zone. As a former member of the *Bürgerschaft* (local parliament), and after he recreates and now leads the Social-Democrat SPD regional organization, your *Vati* is in a mediator situation between the British military administration and German civil offices. Whence the problem of the English language that your father hardly speaks. For this reason, starting May 1, 1946, the SPD Party will hire you as an interpreter. You will accompany your father and other political leaders during their necessary contacts with the British Military Governor and his collaborators. It even seems that some personal, rather hearty relations will be woven between your family and some of them.

Heymannstrasse 6 in 1948

On March 1, 1947, your family at last comes out of temporary conditions and can rent an apartment—which, by the way, I also shall know. It is located on the third upper floor at *Lida-Gustava-Heymannstrasse* 6, in a rather calm neighborhood west of downtown, not too far from *Hallerstrasse*.

A product, as it seems to me, of the intense after-war rebuild activity; it is a large five-upper-story living block out of dark-red bricks, with attic windows between steep tiles and an abundant wine vegetation on its façades. Small lawn surfaces in front, behind low brick walls overhung by small hedges. On the opposite, an unused property; on the backside a playground for children. At the end of the street, the elevated urban railroad; a little further, one of the numerous canals of Hamburg, which is among the many 'Venices of the North' (Amsterdam, Bruges, Stockholm...).

Modern comfort is provided, except central heating. In the beginning, you will have to be content with the coal oven and stay in the kitchen during the winter. Your brother and you now have separate bedrooms, in addition to your parents' room. One particular will surprise me later: the slot in the front door, through which every morning the postman will throw the mail on the corridor floor.

Rémy

Rémy *in 1947*

Apparently, you have not abandoned your dream of taking care of children in England or France. As a member of a group of young Germans in August 1946 near Zurich in Switzerland, you attend an international training session about advanced pedagogy, conducted by the Hamburg pedagogue Anna Siemsen.

In this immediate post-war period with closed borders, it is a welcome opportunity to leave Germany and meet with foreign people.

In the group from France, there is *Rémy*, a young Auschwitz survivor, over-sensitive, enormously angry toward Germany. In the favorable environment of common activities, around a camp fire, singing and playing music, you will succeed in taming his German-antagonistic rage. Your charm, your soft kindness, your talent will do the rest.

In this young man from a Jewish family with Polish roots, which was badly severed by the racist mass murder, you awake the conscience that not all Germans were Hitler-friends, that many of them suffered from the Nazis, that among them there also were—according to one of his usual expressions—'*des gens bien*' (decent people).

In February through March 1947, you participate with two young men as the Hamburg delegation at a congress in London, that takes place on the invitation of the Independent Labour Party, aiming at "United Socialist States of Europe."

London, February 1947, Grete with Heinz-Joachim Heydorn and Wilhelm Dittmer as the German Delegation

Our family archive contains a large photograph of the three of you, as well as a newspaper clip about the event.

However, it is no easy thing at that time to travel abroad. You are not a citizen of a state anymore but belong to the population of an occupied territory. Therefore, no passport but merely a 'military travel permit,' only valid for one journey. And, for getting it, a whole file must be provided, with the evidence that you never belonged to any National-Socialist organization. The only one you indicate is the Students' Union; your membership there probably was required to be admitted in college, certainly not by conviction. I imagine that your father, with his good relations with the British authorities, has facilitated the authorization. I keep your travel permit in my family archive, bearing the identity photograph I chose to illustrate the cover of this book.

So, you cross the North Sea by ship via Bremerhaven; you spend your time in London and in Scotland at friends'. You are so private that neither in your diary kept during this journey nor in the one of your training camp in Switzerland do you mention the bonds you have knotted with *Rémy*.

Merely a tiny clue: in your Great Britain diary you inserted a note with train and ferry schedules between Le Mans, where your lover is living and working, and London. Nothing more. To find tracks of your affair, one must search in your correspondence. Not in your letter exchange after the travel to Switzerland, though.

You certainly have kept these letters; they must have been in my father's archive that was 'forgotten' along with some other items in the cellar, during *Rémy* and Magali's last home move in 1989.

But your parents' archive I inherited includes several explicit statements. The carbon copy of a letter dated December 21, 1946 and January 7, 1947, sent to a certain Gerold, probably the Gerold Meyer, evoked in your letter dated December 31, organizer or leader of the pedagogic training in Switzerland, reveals that *Rémy* has invited you to a 1947 summer working period with him in Le Mans as children educators. On January 22, a letter sent by *Rémy* to your mother confirms this invitation.

On April 10, a letter draft of hers with her confirmed approval of your marriage project. Further, there is the carbon copy of your letter, dated April 18, to the French Socialist MP Salomon Grumbach, an acquaintance of your father's, in which you beg him to lend weight regarding your filed request for immigration and marriage authorization. In this document, you indicate that *Rémy* and you have carried on with exchanging letters after you met in Switzerland, and that he had seized the occasion of your stay in London to spend a few days with you—crossing the French-German border was nearly impossible in those times—and that you have made there the decision to marry.

Finally, there is the carbon copy of a similar letter in French, of which I identified the receiver, whom you met during the London Congress, as Simon Wichené, the Secretary General of the *Confédération Générale des Internés, Déportés politiques de la Résistance* (General Confederation of Imprisoned, Political Deportees of the Resistance). You remind him of his promise to have the relevant authority accelerate the treatment of your request, and you describe your project of constructing a new life for this man who has suffered so much by German guilt.

Emigrant

Well, now your future is decided in accordance with your long-standing project; you will come to France, marry the man you love and help educate Holocaust orphans, with the generous but indeed symbolic idea of trying to make amends to the evil some of your compatriots did.

At that time, your future husband still is in Le Mans, working in an orphanage of the *Œuvre de Secours aux Enfants* (Children Aid Organization, OSE) at Méhoncourt Castle, under the chief educator Lotte Schwarz, who almost adopted him as her foster son. I shall report in detail about his biography in the second *"Rémy"* chapter further down. As I just said, both of them have invited you to join them during the summer of 1947.

However, this is not how things will work. First, you will have to wait for your visa as long as until November. And second, Lotte will be transferred to an OSE home for teenagers located 5 *Rue Rollin*, in the 5th Paris municipal District, close to the *Place de la Contrescarpe* in the Latin Quarter. One of these houses dating from the early seventeenth century with leaning façades, uneven walls, and floors. It is said to be a former monastery. *Rémy* followed her there.

This is where one morning in mid-November 1947 you will end up after a night sitting on board the *Nord-Express* from Hamburg to Paris North train station via Belgium. A trip, by the way, I'll make back and forth so often in my own life, either on my own, or with adults, my sister or my half-brother.

Anyway, you, *Maman Grète*, arrive at the orphanage with a heavy suitcase in each hand, containing your most indispensable belongings. You discover Paris based at *Rue Rollin* and you are excited.

You compare this new metropolis with the ones you have known before. You are surprised by thousands of little details peculiar to Paris or France. You make pretty little freehand drawings with your fountain pen, of the view from your room looking over *Rue Monge* and draw little sketches to illustrate your descriptions.

The legally mandatory banns must have been published in advance, because as early as three or four days after your arrival, you and *Rémy* are married on Thursday, November 20, 1947 at a quarter past eleven, in the townhall of the fifth Paris District facing the *Panthéon*. By necessity, it is *Rémy* who has to provide the witnesses: his elder brother Camille and his 'pseudo-Mother' Lotte. No parents: yours cannot come from Hamburg; his had been murdered in Auschwitz.

By this quick acting, you preserve morality and good manners; therefore you can live together in one of the rooms located in the youth home placed under the supervision of Lotte and *Rémy*. Your marriage meal with your family-in-law will be your first feast '*à la française*,' whereas in Hamburg they still have to struggle for the most necessary goods. To you it was—as they say in Germany—living like God in France.

Immediately afterwards, on Wednesday, November 26, you are naturalized French. For that, as far as I am informed, you have to abandon you German citizenship. One year later, you will be proud of your first passport, a French one. Even though culturally you remain strongly attached to your Northern-German roots, you will strongly feel included in this French society that you have chosen.

However, you never will find a real pleasure in slurping oysters nor overcome your disgust. I do feel like you, by the way, with basically all shellfish and crustacean.

Rejected

You describe life at the *Rue Rollin* home as interesting and multicultural. You also can enjoy your brand-new marriage. "I am playing my husband's wife," you write on December 3. You give *Rémy* German lessons; he plays the clown by inventing pseudo-German sentences; you kill yourselves laughing.

During this same month of December 1947, a rebellion is building up against you, 'the German,' lead by a few of the toughest youngsters, the Buchenwald survivors. Although you are merely their educator's wife, they declare an absolute refusal to live under one roof with you. According to your December 31 letter, Lotte and *Rémy* supposedly had discussed too much with the boys instead of letting the case ebb by itself, so that the *frondeurs* could not go back without losing face.

In spite of the support from two other orphanages, the OSE managers first "wound and turned themselves," then let you know it would be better if *Rémy* could resign. Not a courageous standpoint, in your opinion, in fear American donators could become angered. Be that as it may, your husband gives in and now both of you are at end of year in search of an employment. You live with Camille 15 *Rue Bargue* in the 15th Paris District, the former home of *Rémy's* parents.

Grète and Rémy Rue Bargue, Christmas 1947

You can the more content yourself with this decision than you think that Lotte's personality is a little too strong and authoritarian. It is all right with you to keep some distance with her. In my own opinion, she indeed was the kind of person who better knows than yourself what is good for you and not easily accepts any points of view differing from hers. Because, while, unfortunately, I hardly had time to know you, I did know her quite well.

After all, your situation is not so bad, because open jobs are not lacking; you will have up to four position offers at your disposal.

You make up your minds in favor of the one of them that enables your soonest beginning and your working together as a couple. It was issued by *La Table Ronde* (The Round Table), a society supported by unions and the Ministry of Health, which takes care of children in difficult situations. As early as in mid-January, you live and work in your new home, in Nivillers Castle near Beauvais, north of Paris.

Here you are not dealing with Holocaust orphans from the Jewish Community but with hardship cases and former convicts. Both of you will not stand it more than a single month because you do not like the place. The children are far too unbalanced, loud, from naughty to brutal, in short: unbearable.

You complain about the many bed wetters. Poor you! Of course you cannot know your own son would have to suffer from the same symptom. You will not be there anymore for it.

Regarding the nasty children of Nivillers: *Rémy's* progressive educational methods remain without effects on them; the role of a warden does not suit him. Moreover, your colleagues are not particularly pleasant, the rooms poorly heated, running water is often missing, and you are too busy to take care of your laundry and room cleaning. The only positive aspect for you: in various situations you realize that you are dealing well with the French language, particularly when it comes to understanding what is spoken.

Well, all for naught this time. But failures too teach lessons. Now at least you both know what you do not like. So, back to job offers and to *Rue Bargue* in this second half of February 1948.

UJRE-CCE, Nice

You reject another proposal about a position as chief educator in *Auvergne* Region, in the *Massif Central* mountains, because it only concerns *Rémy*. You remain in expectation of a third possibility. The answer comes early in March, positive.

Your employer will be the *Commission Centrale de l'Enfance* (Central Commission for Children, CCE), a department of the *Union des Juifs pour la Résistance et l'Entraide* (Union of Jews for Resistance and Mutual Aid, UJRE), an organization issued from the Communist Resistance.

In your letter dated March 5, 1948, you are excited about the perspective of a small orphanage above Nice with thirty normal Jewish children with *Rémy* as their chief educator. In mid-March the time has come. You have moved from the cold Picardy to the warm spring sun of the French Riviera.

Now probably begins one of the happiest portions of your life. Your letter dated March 30, 1948, reflects your delight. You had arrived a fortnight before to prepare the Villa named *Domaine de Beauregard*, and located 240-242 *Avenue de Pessicart* 240-242. The four hundred steps leading down into town reveal how high above your location is and how magnificent the view on city, countryside and Mediterranean Sea.

Enthusiastically, you make with your fountain pen a pretty drawing of the terrace with house corner, palm trees, balustrade and panorama. Just an allusive sketch but one thinks to be there. In your following letter dated April 7, you draw with colored pencils the room you have furnished for yourselves.[13]

Enhancing your happiness, still fully in your honeymoon, you are expecting your first child to be born in fall.

Grète and Rémy *in the streets of Nice, on April 28, 1948*

Late in March, the home counts its seventeen first little inhabitants, of which the youngest is three and a half. In mid-April, thirteen more are coming. They were all entrusted to the CCE because their families could not provide for them, most of them having had one or both parents murdered in the Nazi camps. Most of these children come from

---

[13] See "Documents" section, #22-23.

the orphanage in Sainte-Maxime, also by the Mediterranean Sea, not far from Saint-Tropez. The older ones supervise the younger ones.

After the Easter vacation, they go to school, down the four hundred steps, escorted by *Rémy*. For your part, you are in charge of the little ones, the six- to eight-year-olds. You help them do their school work. Compared with the Nivillers ones, you discover intelligent children with good will in spite of their being behind, caused by chaotic school attendance and emotional troubles.

They have a great need for tenderness and affection and will receive them from you, *Maman Grète*. *Rémy* plays more the paternal role with sports, constructions, educational games and so on. Both of you open their minds to reading, music and arts. You often seek advice from your husband who is more experienced in educational matters.

Your everyday life gets organized to your great satisfaction, both of you. You give a detailed report about it.

The Nice terrace: Peeling potatoes with Grète (arrow) playing on her accordion

You very seldom evoke a child by name. The only one in this case in Nice is a little *Mischa*, who was born during the battle of Stalingrad. Since a photograph shows you affectionately holding this little boy in your arms, I am convinced that my own name Michel and my nickname *Micha* will be chosen by you in memory of him. I told him that, by the way, because, although he is living in the USA, I was lucky enough to meet with him, as well as with his very kind sister Esther, who lives in Paris and can be seen in the same picture.

Esther (left) and Micha Brym (on Grète's lap), Nice 1948

You already mention vacation plans. You would love to get back to Hamburg, see again your family and introduce *Rémy*. But it will not be possible in that year, because as recent employees you will not be entitled to enough days off, because in summer your pregnancy will have progressed too far, and because you have to dedicate yourselves full-time to the CCE home children. Well, next time, then. You do not know it yet but you still will have to wait for two more years before your project can succeed.

Meanwhile, a first heavy ordeal will strike your couple. Around May 20, 1948, in your fifth month, you lose the little boy you were expecting. On May 23, you write that you are recovering fast, that you should have spared yourself more around Pentecost, that this incident will not prevent you from getting the three children you wish to have, and that next time you will be more careful.

Did *Rémy* provide you with the black kitten named

Mickey as a comfort? Unfortunately, it will not survive long and you will have a little striped Muschi. I wonder where it might come from that I in turn shall be so fond of cats.

The lovers, Nice, July 1948

Nice is an experimental orphanage in the sense that the CCE is financed by local donators instead of using centrally or even internationally collected contributions, like from the US-American 'Joint' (American Jewish Joint Distribution Committee), a Jewish solidarity organization, if I understand correctly. Because of this, you and the children are requisitioned for participating in small performances for the wealthier Jews of Nice. However, in spite of all efforts, this formula will not turn out to be successful.

Very soon a poor financial situation occurs. Your wages are only partly paid, sometimes with delays, sometimes even borrowed back to provide your home with food or utensils. So eventually, after it had been used during the particularly hot summer as a vacation camp, the orphanage must be closed for the new school year beginning in fall.

Andrésy

On August 15, 1948, you write that the children know nothing yet about the closure project and that your future has not yet been decided. You will be transferred either to the Alps, near the Swiss border, or to the Paris area. In the former case it would be to a mysterious location you never had heard of before; you spell it "Exleben", as it sounds in your ears.

Mountains, winter sports … this was rather appealing, but to be near the capital with its attractions, as well as 'your' apartment in *Rue Bargue*, would not displease you either.

Anyway, it is the latter option that comes true, as you report on September 6 to Hamburg. With one part of your children you travel late in September to Andrésy, approximately twenty-five kilometers (sixteen miles) west of Paris. The remaining part travels to … Aix-les-Bains, a spa at a mountain lake in Savoy.

You all—cat included—travel by railroad. You do not know it yet, but every annual school beginning will lead to a home move, this one like the next three ones.

Andrésy on the one hand means the end of the Mediterranean magic, of the quasi-mystic 'Orient' that you had encountered in Nice; it is not anymore this kind of family house started and operated by both of you.

On the other hand, it is a beautiful and large park estate around the famous *Manoir de Denouval*, called by you the

Castle, overlooking the Seine River, on which you see the passing barges, providing you with a longing for travels, for the Berlin lakes, rivers, and canals. It also means your closeness to plants in the park, the transforming of which you will follow in the course of the seasons, captivated.

It also means to become part of a larger pedagogic team which also includes another couple, Pierre and Zette Lunet, as well as—at least in the beginning—Lotte Schwarz. But this time you are not under her command, since she is in charge of awakening the children in educational, artistic and cultural fields, as well as 'public relations' towards the many visitors, often donators.

For six weeks, that is from September 20 to November 9, 1948, your correspondence is discontinued, whereas normally you would write nearly once a week. Your parents are concerned; your *Vati* tries to get news through his SPD fellow Max Cohen-Reuss who lives in Paris. Consequently, you explain your *Mutti* and *Vati* that all is well, you just could not find the time to write because of your adaption to your new life, of the pedagogic meetings precisely held in the evening at the time when you would write your mail, of the Sundays spent, on *Rémy*'s request, taking the train to Paris and going to the movies, the theaters, or other activities.

You both pay a visit, practically on command, to Cohen-Reuss. Like a good boy, Max writes his report on November 1948. He describes you as fresh and merry, and *Rémy* as trustworthy. You love each other, have much to do and you like your work. There is no reason to be concerned for you, that is his opinion.

That is all well and good but, as they say, there is no smoke without fire. Did you not omit to write the least little post card for one month and a half? Knowing your further history, I cannot but imagine a little crisis of depression. The alienist who took care of you in 1941 in Berlin did consider you as 'manic depressive,' what nowadays would be called 'bipolar.' Meaning an alternation between 'excited' and 'dejected.'

I am convinced that in 1948, as young as twenty-five, with a recently begun self-chosen career, with the experience of your great love, far more often 'up' than 'down.' But this here might be one of your few 'ebbs.'

The reasons for it can be guessed. Perhaps, with a delay, the consequences of losing your first baby, probably also the disappointment to have left so soon the Mediterranean enchantments, the end of a beautiful summer and the incoming winter. You also experience several room switches within the castle, as well as a slightly overloaded daily schedule, whence strain and lack of sleep. Each of these causes might more or less have played a role.

Be that as it may, you eventually become accustomed to your new circumstances and everything is right again: *"We now understand that we get better rest if from time to time we spend our day off reading and resting at the orphanage."*

You describe your everyday life. Finally, you are pleased with the way you work together with *Rémy*. Both of you are in charge of one group of nine- to twelve-year-old children and you share the various tasks. Additionally, you are a temporary carer for the youngest, when needed.

On December 12, 1948, you report that David, *Rémy's* seventeen-year-old brother, has joined you as an educator. With the older ones, the eighteen-year-olds, it was not all right but with the younger ones it is. The strange thing is that not one of the former Andrésy children I met could remember David was present. You cannot have invented it! You even will tell that in summer 1949 he will be a supervisor in a summer camp near the Spanish border (probably Tarnos by the Atlantic Coast), but on this point neither could I find anyone remembering it, nor any clue in any document apart from your letters. Strange indeed…

What you also benefit from is the Christmas vacation, your first real vacation since you are working together as a married couple. You spend it in your *Rue Bargue* home, together with Monique, *Rémy's* little sister, who just became twelve. After a feast with champagne, orphanage life resumes.

On January 17, 1949, you deliver many details. You like your room in the home pretty well: small but with running hot water. For Hannukah there had been a great celebration with performances in Yiddish language.

You lead a weaving, sewing, and bast fiber workshop, to which a photograph attests. *Rémy* is in charge of pottery and joinery. Each of these activities occupies a dozen children, once a week.

The winter is mild: 10 degrees Celsius (50 Fahrenheit). Many children stay in bed with influenza but the two of you are spared. You also write: "Life with the children now is becoming more and more pleasant. We have got used to one another, they already trust in us much more, we have done and experienced things together." What is this? You had not mentioned it. Perhaps it happened during the six weeks without a letter and could be one more reason for your 'down' in last fall.

During the common evening washing, you would play on your violin and *Rémy* on his recorder. A French proverb says that music pacifies manners. You write that Lotte has resigned from her job to prevent "Pierre" (Pierre Lunet?) from losing his, because she likes him too much to take the chance. She has found another position with a government-controlled authority for orphan villages.

You seem to be in a good phase, because you explain you are constantly rejoicing that you made the right choice for your life. You feel in good shape and fit for your task. In retrospect, I think that Andrésy was the climax of your educator career, the period in which you can fully apply your talents. Thereafter you for sure will strongly have regretted that things were not anymore as they used to be.

Pregnancy

On Monday, February 7, 1949, you report digestive problems, a probable pregnancy. As opposed to Nice, you will be able to get good rest since you share a children group with your husband. Moreover—so I say—here are not the four hundred steps to climb. All is well.

You earn then ten thousand francs a month (with free food, lodging, and laundry); your brother-in-law Camille earns as a skilled worker between twenty and twenty-five thousand francs. You don't tell if your husband gets the same wages as you.

As early as on February 10, you confirm you are expecting a baby. Your parents wrote they were surprised by your general satisfaction. You too, you say, but you do feel better and freer. You better control now a world that was foreign to you. You achieve projects instead of just planning. Be it only that you earn money and convert it into beautiful and useful things. That is something new for you.

This is how you share your wages: each of you has one quarter of the total at his or her disposal and the other half goes into your common fund.

You have a new hairstyle: your hair "for several months not put up anymore, but framing my face, with a permanent wave and combed to the back." In shops, people think you are a child and address you as "well, little girl." "Family fate," you say. Like in your mother's case, your youthful look and short stature are deceptive.

That sounds familiar to me, too. For decades, I even had been wearing a beard, so that inattentive persons would not address me as *"Bonjour, Madame"* without themselves being ridiculous. Now, as a retired man, and shaved, I am rather satisfied with my younger look, just as *Mutti* used to be.

And how did you speak? You do not say anything about it, of course. Some of your former foster children told me that you had a melodic voice, sang nicely and had a slight and soft German accent. Some of them did not even remember you had an accent at all. This is surprising if one takes into consideration that you only had been in France for a single year. You must indeed have been highly gifted with languages.

On Wednesday, April 13, 1949, off to the Easter vacation. With twelve home children you camp in Burgundy, in the Morvan Mountains, near Settons Lake. Your stay goes well. You are making plans for the summer which actually will not be performed. In this year, once more, Hamburg will be dropped but you do not know it yet. On Tuesday, May 3, you proudly report your first passport. One more year will pass before you can make use of it. You do not yet know this either.

For the time being, you take part in a mass meeting of the World Conference for Peace; you make preparations for the first Exhibition for Peace of the Movement against Racism, Anti-Semitism and for Peace (MRAP).

You also have much to organize so that many of 'your' children can be summer guests of foreign families.

You pass your days off at *Rue Bargue* ("…it is too funny

to play the married couple in our apartment"), because your usual life really is not typical. The rhythm is given by the life of the children you are in charge of.

Your body weight beats every record, you write. Choosing a given name for your first child is on your agenda. In those days, of course, no ultrasound images were available yet, therefore both genders must be provided for. For a girl you already have chosen *Catia* (Anna-Katherine), possible abbreviation: *Anka*. For a boy, you still are excluding Marco, Guy, Romain, Jacques, Jean, Joseph and Adolf. Why especially these ones (except the latter...)? I shall be damned if I know.

On June 19, a travel schedule for your *Mutti* is taking shape. She would come from September 7 to early October and be at your side to assist you for your first maternity. *Rémy*, for his part, will escort a group of children for six weeks in London and take his summer vacation from late August to October 1. Your maternity leave will be granted from July 15 at least to October 1, depending on the actual birth date.

Your female cat Muschi has had kittens and disappeared. You get a new pussy, Djiki, so tiny that it can "sleep in *Rémy's* hand," but which you will not mention anymore.

Then occurs a rather restless period of time in which you try to obtain an accommodation for yourself in London, with the help of your *Vati* and his connections because you would like to join *Rémy* there. Eventually, the CCE will refuse to approve your journey, on the grounds that your husband is to fully dedicate himself to supervising the children entrusted to him. This was not such a bad decision, finally, since the summer will be particularly hot, and you spend at Denouval Park a very pleasant time of calm and rest, even if in the end you will miss your husband. Before departing to their vacation, around forty children sleep outside the building, in large tents. Afterwards, you will remain among adults, with only a very small number of remaining children.

Catia

On Tuesday, August 23, 1949, you mention the managing lady, from Lithuania, same age as your *Mutti*, who is looking forward to seeing her. Your mother will be allowed to live in the small janitor house at the park gate. Interestingly, you also mention the lady's daughter, Betty, who is very attached to *Rémy* and part of the London group. You hold an intense correspondence with the children accommodated abroad.

On Sunday, August 27, you inform your parents that you forgot to announce the passing through Hamburg of the train bringing back one of your groups from Norway. They could have gone to the station and caught sight of some French Jewish children. But, you say, "they do not look otherwise than any ordinary people."

Afterwards, your correspondence is discontinued. Fully normal since your *Mutti* came visiting you. For her it means discovering France, Paris, Denouval, it means meeting *Rémy* and the children you are taking care of.

Your delivery will take place at a clinic[14] in Poissy where she visits you daily by bicycle or by bus.

---

[14] In France, a *clinique* (I translate 'clinic') is a private smaller hospital, as opposed to a large public hospital (*hôpital*).

Catia *in* Rémy'*s arms, happy* Papa

The 'happy event' occurs on September 18, 1949, at two o'clock in the night. It is a girl. She is declared at the civil registration office by *Rémy* with the given names *Catherine Anne* instead of *Anne-Catherine* as you intended. Either the two of you changed your minds or the declarant, exhausted after a sleepless night, made a slip, or else played a trick on you. I do not know. I prefer the former explanation. Be it as it may, it is over with the intended pet name, *Anka*.

There only remains *Catia*, spelled *Katja* when you write in German. Much later, after having been a teenager, her nickname will be further abbreviated in *Cat*. *Anne*, for its part, is a tribute to Anna Judith (*Aniouta/Anjuta*, later *Aniou*), the daughter of Lotte Schwarz. *Aniou* and you seem to be good friends. At that time, she is studying medicine and will later become a bone surgeon. I also notice that both your *Oma* and your *Mutti* have *Anna* as their first or middle names.

Catia's arrival on this Earth is everything but sailing in calm waters. Indeed, on August 10, 1949, you already wrote that it is the turn of the Andrésy orphanage to be closed. As usual for financial reasons: In this period of McCarthyism, the US-American Joint stops its donations to the CCE, seen as a Communist organization. And because the large building is difficult to heat, it swallows every day a ton of coal, an expense of eleven thousand francs. A huge sum compared with the ten thousand of your monthly salary. For a while, by the way, the furnace only was lit on days when the children had showers. Moreover, the orphanage needs too many personnel.

So, it is shut and its inhabitants distributed between two smaller children homes in Le Raincy, this time in the eastern Paris suburban area, completely opposite Andrésy. Pierre Lunet becomes the chief educator of the 'taller' ones at *Avenue des Coteaux* and *Rémy* chief educator of the 'smaller' ones at 18 *Allée du Plateau.*

You regret that you again will have to wipe small running noses like in Nice, instead of carrying on with your present group. You even wonder if you should change occupations, but at the same time you think that the orphanage life suits the two of you.

Considering the circumstances, you have to deal simultaneously with your mother's presence, *Catia's* arrival on Earth, your home move and your settling in Le Raincy. I hardly dare to imagine these 'crazy days.' Additionally, general strain, including *Rémy*, just back from his stay in the heat of London.

Le Raincy (1)

The so-called *Raincy-Plateau* orphan home is simply a detached house with two upper floors and a garden.

Raincy-Plateau children home, drawing by Mutti, *August 1952, pencil and fountain pen with blue ink*

You get well along with the managing lady, *Fée*, whom you describe as very kind. Your baby is your full-time occupation; you breast-feed her. On Wednesday, October 12, 1949, you write that the person acting in replacement for you is to come on the next day for one month, "a former Andrésy male educator whom we know well and like." As a result of my research, it might have been a certain Isard.

Rémy is occupied with a lot of do-it-yourself work to improve your furnishings; fortunately, he is gifted for it.

In your letter dated November 14, you report that your deputy remains at your place and you have a half-time employment, earning five thousand five hundred francs a month, added to the thirteen thousand earned by *Rémy* and your baby benefit of thirteen hundred. Now we know it: your husband earns more than you—but, indeed, he is a chief educator.

At least, thanks to these conditions, you are free to participate only in the activities you like and you can optimize the time you dedicate to your child, who is calm and healthy. At the end of November, you both undertake the furnishing, equipment, and decoration of the 'club,' a hut in the backside garden, intended for leisure activities of the children.

Sensational: you are preparing for your brother's visit for the holiday season. After mother-in-law and son-in-law, both brothers-in-law will at last meet. And you will be able to see each other again after a couple of years.

I forgot to mention that upon each border-crossing travel you are most concerned with the question of visas, currency exchange, and international train tickets. In those post-war years, nothing is simple.

The season will turn out to be a happy period but in the end there will be a phase of such a weariness that your correspondence only resumes on February 2. You explain your exhaustion with your breast-feeding causing a lack of calcium which you combat by means of calcium pills.

Resignation or dismissal? You do not reveal in which way you stop working for the CCE. In case some day I can access the personnel files of the CCE, maybe I can find out.

You say it is a relief to be able to dedicate yourself full-time to *Catia*. But since you have free food and accommodation you will carry on with directing the activities you like on a volunteer basis, that is, choir singing and handicraft.

Nonetheless, it was a breaking point for you: you stop earning your own living. And I think this is the beginning of your 'descent to hell': irregular, with ups and downs. But by and by—almost imperceptibly—come together all ingredients of the cocktail that will lead to your end; I shall later come back to it.

In the meantime, you get a proposal that might have pleased both of you. Through Lotte, you were put in contact with the pedagogue Ernst Jablonski, also known as *Jouhi*, who is searching for teachers for his children home named *La Forge* in the southern Paris suburb Fontenay-aux-Roses. You visit the premises but the two of you are hesitating because the children there have many problems. The subject will not be picked up again later.

May 1, 1950: Grète singing, Daniel Baron (with black ribbon) and more children from Le Raincy-Plateau

The spring of 1950 is particularly hot. Also regarding politics: On May 1, you report that you have entrusted *Catia* to *Fée*, so you could take part with the children in the demonstration, the outside temperature being around 30 degrees Celsius (around 85 degrees Fahrenheit). You all are singing and showing a board with a slogan against remilitarizing Germany: "Do not allow rearming our parents' executioners." There remains a photograph in which you are marching and singing with the children.

You also tell that you are sewing clothes, to special prices for friends. For making your own garments, you draw sketches from shop windows at *Champs-Élysées* Avenue.

Once more you are seized by a great desire to spend your summer vacation in Hamburg. But this time it seems to take shape. You want to travel from August 15 to September 15. And like every end of school year there is a rumor of closing the orphanage, as you write on May 9, 1950; decision awaited within a week.

For the time being, the children wake up without their educators' help, using a couple of alarm clocks that were donated to them. In June, they participate in four solemn performances intended to raise interest of Jewish circles for your children's homes. Besides, you regret that many Jews stay by themselves and hardly speak French, even when they have been living in France for a very long time.

Summer vacations are approaching; the departure of some children is delayed, caused by an outbreak of measles; they even had to be brought back from the train station by taxi and put in quarantine. This time, *Rémy* will not travel away with children but stay in Le Raincy until your own vacation.

Meanwhile, you enjoy house and garden with cock, twenty chickens and five hens, which lay exactly the number of eggs you need for your daily usage. Ten children did not travel away because they were chosen for playing in a motion picture, a little girl even as a main character. Film director is Louis Daquin and the title is *Maître Après Dieu* (Master after God, literally).

My family archive contains a series of photographs of this 1950 first summer vacation in Hamburg and Kiel, with *Catia* who just learns to walk. Now, *Rémy* is able to make acquaintance with your homeland and all your relatives, your *Vati*, your *Oma*, your uncles and aunts. He makes a good impression on all of them and *Catia* enchants them.

After this homeland visit, connecting your old and new

lives, you return invigorated, cheerful, and energy laden to France.

Livry-Gargan

It is the better because the inevitable home move awaits you. This time it is not far, because Livry-Gargan, 81 *Avenue du Colonel-Fabien* is almost next door.

Former Livry-Gargan children's home in 2012

The house is larger, more beautiful and more pleasant, you say, and you are allocated a larger apartment on the second upper floor. I did a pilgrimage to the place in 2012. The house is still there, red and grey, with a few front steps and long balconies, even though the grounds have narrowed to make room for new schools and the concrete railings imitating tree branches were replaced with modern ones.

The building is owned by the municipality and put at the disposal of the French Red Cross for the accommodation of their charity activities, such as sorting and storing donated garments. As opposed to Andrésy, for a long period nothing memorialized the Jewish Holocaust orphans taken care of here. The users of the house were not aware of the fact. On Sunday, April 30, 2017, at last, an official plaque was inaugurated by town officials, Holocaust victim societies, and former CCE orphans.

So, with Raincy-Plateau, the CCE has once more to give up a children's home, although the organization remains owner of the house, as we shall see one year later, but—shh!—you still know nothing about it.

You like to be in your new home; Rose, the manager was born in Russia—*Fée* is on maternity leave—the cook is from Spain and an Anarchist. So is his food.

Catia runs around and amuses the children very much, even though several among them do not remember her. Memory is selective. This happy little girl having her parents perhaps is conflicting too much with their own orphan history.

Catia *and Grète in Livry-Gargan in 1951*

You, *Maman Grète*, do not say if you have been again a CCE employee. I am surprised that, with *Rémy,* you have in charge a large part of the children's everyday life. In late October, you even will be acting for the manager while she has bronchitis. On a volunteer base, how devoted! *Catia* spends a couple of hours daily at the home of a neighbor, *Madame Madeleine* whom you pay for it.

In November you are worried about your *Mutti*, who is depressed, making mountains of molehills. In June already you were concerned about your *Vati*, now a member of the

Bundestag,[15] who, strained after two journeys abroad, was injured at night in a car accident. Even from such a distance, you feel responsible for your parents.

You spend pleasant season holidays at the turn of the year. The Easter vacation in the second half of April occurs in common with thirteen nine- to sixteen-year-old protégés in Chaponval, a district of Auvers-sur-Oise (where the painter Van Gogh ended his life). Additionally, there is the cook and a little dog named Pif. Because of a general strike in public transport and energy, it is your vegetable provider who brings you all there in his truck.

The cottage, you say, is fashionable and comfortable, you feel good and you like the food. But the weather is rather cold. There too I did a pilgrimage to have a look. The location is calm, in spite of the nearby railroad tracks. The tow path offers nice stroll possibilities along the Oise, a tributary river of the Seine.

You still do not know yet if in summer you will again travel to Germany or if the Germans will come and see you. On Wednesday, May 9, you report that *Catia* is going to have "a sibling": that is I. You feel better than ever; I guess it is the effect of the maternity hormones, my first present for you. Both of you are happy about a second child. It is all right by me: at least I was desired.

Now your plans are established: you will again travel to Hamburg in August–September. *Rémy* will have the greatest difficulties obtaining precise vacation date information from

---

[15] Lower house of the Federal German parliament, together with the *Bundesrat*, upper house representing the *Länder* (states).

the CCE, till the last moment, by the way.

You tell that Lotte now works with *Madame Maurette* (I never heard her being called differently; did the lady perhaps have no given name?[16]), founder of the International School Geneva. Commissioned by the UNESCO, the two of them travel all around the country, driving a vehicle fitted as a library.

Regarding your children's home, the manager Rose is very kind but technically not competent. Everything goes wrong, you say, and the central management has commissioned *Rémy* to write a report about the situation.

To please the sponsors, the children are learning the Hebraic alphabet; you join them, out of pure curiosity. You also give two foreigners English lessons, as well as German homework help to René, a sixteen-year-old Fleming with good dispositions. About mid-June, a great spring *fête* is to be organized.

According to your letter dated May 3, 1951, it appears that your *Vati* has entered into bad relations with the Hamburg SPD, and that moreover your parents are in such couple problems that you envisage a separate home for your *Mutti*, which did not occur but nonetheless makes you worry very much.

On your part, you have become politically active, passionately. After having long asserted that your political education was insufficient, that you would come into trouble in political discussions, three and a half years after your immi-

---

[16] From recent research, I know that her first name was Marie-Thérèse and that she died in 1981 aged 102 years!

gration to France you eventually joined the French Communist Party. You are active in another 'cell'[17] than *Rémy*. He additionally is active in the Movement for Peace.

You find it exciting and instructive to attend the debates at the 'cell,' to approach people in the streets and sell the Party newspaper *L'Humanité*, or going from door to door and collect signatures. Previously, you had a completely different image of Communists. You thought they were full of some mysticism and undermined by Soviet spies. In reality, you find them kind, calm, and with practical skills for their activities. It gives you an indication of how much minds are influenced by capitalist propaganda, you say.

An event has upset you in your letter dated May 23. You were attending a mass meeting at the *Vel d'Hiv* indoor Velodrome. Just a remark: you do not allude to the role this place played in the abduction of Jews, including your parents-in-law in 1942. Anyway, you have been there, together with Pierre Lunet and around ten children. You listened to the communist political leader Jacques Duclos, who was giving his opening speech for the election campaign.

Upon exiting the building, indescribable confusion. Two tear gas grenades had been thrown, supposedly by De Gaulle supporters, you say. In the next morning, you read in *L'Humanité* that the security forces had discovered and disarmed a couple of bombs half an hour before the event. They were powerful enough to blow up the whole building.

You all fear the beginning of a fascist dictatorship in

---

[17] Smallest local organization unit, where members have regular meetings

France and you are studying possible refuges, Hamburg for instance.

You are engaged in an intense correspondence before the approaching summer vacation. The plan to have your brother-in-law Camille travel with you will fail from his part. *Rémy* would like to travel from Hamburg to Berlin and attend the International Youth Peace Days. Once on the spot he will give up because of tiredness.

Your *Vati* is on a health cure on Sylt Island,[18] after having been in surgery for a node on one of his vocal cords—speaker's disease. A politician, a passionate speaker like him, being forced to shut up! At his request you make preparations for spending the beginning of your vacation with him.

Apart from this, a donator has given the Livry-Gargan orphanage some sand for a jumping pit. *Catia* is getting a foretaste of beach life. Because of your pregnancy—my fault—you, however, will have to refrain from swimming in the sea. Sorry!

Due to the great mess at the children's home, you have started a vast cleaning-up operation. *Rémy* sends an ultimatum to the central management about the home manager, Rose. It is either she or you. You have a second sleeping room for your accommodation, almost too nice to be true. Do not worry, you will see, it will not last long.

Different subject: your intended travelling date is continuously changing. Starting on August 1, at last, time has

---

[18] Popular seaside resort in the North Sea, the most north-western spot in Germany. One of the 'dream locations' of the Meitmann family.

come: off you are. Afterwards, no letters anymore, just another series of photographs, among which many showing *Catia*, less a baby, more a little blonde girl with many relatives all around her.

Rémy is the first to travel back home, you two girls comfortably follow by sleeper on September 15, by taxi from the North Station to your home. The best trip in your life, you write. Later on, one can read between the lines that in Germany you sometimes had to get some rest, knocked down by your condition and the heat. Nevertheless—well, well—I should like to believe you. I think of the myth of Antaeus who would recover his full strength every time he touched his mother Gaia, the Earth. In your homeland, you too may have recovered new forces.

Le Raincy (2)

Back we are in Livry-Gargan. The orphanage is full of plaster and wallpaper rolls. "One man is repapering and repainting every room…" This will not disturb you too long: you hear that the central management has set up in haste a reorganization plan for the children's homes, involving a swap between Pierre Lunet's 'tall ones' and *Rémy*'s 'small ones.' But it creates a problem: the *Raincy-Coteaux* children's home has no suitable service accommodation. The solution found consists of *Rémy* working in the *Coteaux* home while living with his family in the nearby (former) *Plateau* one.

However, upheaval in last minute: the children remain where they are but you live nevertheless in *Allée du Plateau*. At first, the idea seems insane ("First reaction: we roared with laughter. What don't they dare to do with us!"), because it would perfectly have been possible for you—for us—all to live in Livry. And afterwards, after thinking about it, you find the solution not so bad after all, although less advantageous for the CCE since you in person are providing numerous services, such as, for instance, answering telephone calls in absence of the manager or receiving deliveries.

So, "a freight vehicle" comes in the late afternoon of Thursday, September 17, 1951, to carry you and your belongings from Livry-Gargan to Le Raincy. You write that your life away from the noise of a children's home feels like "in a fairy tale." Your husband cycles twice a day between

Allée *du Plateau* and *Avenue du Colonel-Fabien* and back, in eight minutes. Considering the steep slope in between, I wonder which way you are meaning, outward, homeward or an average time. Most likely the best time, that is, from home to work, downhill.

Rémy has lunch in Livry, but he makes an afternoon pause at home while 'his children' are at school. You say you like your sunny apartment on the first upper floor. The space at your disposal has now increased due to the absence of home children. There only remain a janitor, his wife, and their nineteen-month-old daughter, Jacqueline, in the ground floor, as well as two twenty-year-old former home girls on the second upper floor.

You now live like any housewife because you receive neither food nor laundry or heating for free. You have to pay for water, gas and electricity; however, apparently no rent.

Well, you like your new situation; you "look forward with confidence to the new year." I can well imagine that this again is the effect of hormones because your future will look completely different from what you expect.

On October 10, you answer a letter in which your parents seem concerned about the carrying out of your pending second maternity. You reassure them with the description of how everything has been planned. Apparently, you have given up your project of giving birth at the Paris Clinic of Metal Industry Workers, where the latest methods for pain reduction from the USSR are applied. You rather have chosen a birth clinic in the nearby Les Pavillons-sous-Bois, 112 *Avenue Aristide-Briand*, according to my civil registration birth record. On the latter, by the way, my parents' official residence remains in Livry-Gargan, probably because your husband and you did not take the time to make the address change with the authorities.

This time, you do not wish your *Mutti* to be involved for staying at your side. You had rather her visit you in spring, in milder weather, to see her new grandchild. During your stay in clinic, your husband and *Madame Madeleine* will take care of *Catia*. Your daughter, by the way, speaks better and better; she masters German quite as well as French. On October 25, my birth is imminent. *Rémy* begins to be fed up with being alone in charge of around forty children.

Your next letter is dated November 8, written in bed, at the clinic. On Sunday, November 4, 1951, at half past four in the afternoon, a boy, I, was born without any difficulty, whom you provided with the names Michel Alexandre. My usual nickname will be *Micha*, spelled *Mischa* for the Germans. And short *Mich* when I am grown up, as far as I can be called so with my height of one hundred fifty eight centimeters and three quarters, equivalent to five feet, two and a half inches—with so small figures, one really has to be precise.

I already explained that my first name—supposedly—is a reminder of the little Micha from the orphanage in Nice. What I know for sure is that my middle name is a tribute to my father's dear maternal uncle who died two years before and at whose home *Rémy* had been heartily accommodated at his return from the Camps. I also have a first cousin who received 'Alexandre' as his first name for similar reasons.

In the beginning, you breast-feed me, as you did for *Catia*. Later however, you write that you had to stop, without telling the reason. Perhaps because you lose again too much calcium, with it even three teeth. I do not know. Anyway, both of you are pleased with my arrival and "optimism goes on in the Stermann family." *Rémy* also is happy to change occupations soon and to live like an average family man with free evenings, Sundays, and holidays.

On Wednesday, November 21, you write that you and I left the clinic on Wednesday 14. The husband of the midwife and clinic owner (*Monsieur Varoqueaux*, according to my research results), a painting artist, made us the honor and "drove us in person in his automobile named Caroline, which is a noble wreck, to our home. Micha was dozing like Katja, 2 years ago."

You play often with *Catia*, who does not seem very jealous and shows moderate interest for her little brother, except when I am crying. Then, she would say: "*you see, it cries, the doll*" and eventually she weeps too. You describe your new baby: "*Mischa* has rather brown (until now) eyes and scarce, light-colored hair. His suggested nose seems to tend toward *Rémy*."

Resigning from the UJRE-CCE

On Wednesday, December 19, 1951, you clarify my father's resigning from the CCE. He considers himself as underpaid for his responsibilities and for the time he devotes to the orphanage children. He also claimed a compensation for the lost service accommodation in Livry-Gargan and the resulting additional expenses.

I shall rather let you describe in your own words how the central management responded:

> "Allegedly, it was <u>not possible</u> to give *Rémy* what he demanded, and this is the pretext on which *Rémy* then handed in his notice for January 1st. However, he had found a new employment where he was to begin immediately (Dec. 1st). It became a leaving completely out of the blue, but we are not fallen out, they now have invited us as guests to a fete at the children's home.—The children were upset: they have demanded an explanation from the chief 'conductor' lady and claimed that Rémy should remain at the children's home. It was moving to see how much they are attached to *Rémy*. Just the fact that I was away from the orphanage had given them a shock. Now all is over for them, particularly as Rémy's successor gave up after a fortnight and also has gone. There now only remain *Madame* Jeanne (see Andrésy, *Mutti*) and a very young girl. Rémy is just sorry because of the children, but on the whole we are really glad to be off the thing. The women who

are sitting there in the headquarters are neither competent for their work nor above gossip, evil reputation, hatred and jealousy, and they had little knowledge about our work. Additionally, as an educator responsible for 40 children, Rémy was earning less than an unqualified worker. That is, in cash. With accommodation, food, electricity etc. it was much more, of course, but it was nonetheless not adequate for his work. Above all not for his <u>working time</u>. We are tremendously glad that at last we have a real family life. Rémy returns home at 7 in the evening! Saturdays often completely off, otherwise from noon, and then Sundays! Previously, we knew neither weekends nor holidays. He likes his work well. He goes to 4 to 6 people every day, repairs heating and kitchen ovens (gas) and receives often enough 10 DM (800 F) as a daily tip! His fixed salary is 6,000 F per week, that is over 70 marks according to my calculation. But the tipping is significant. Bus and *Metro*[19] tickets are paid by the branch office. Just not his commuting from home to work, naturally. It represents 2,000 F per month. But we get monthly 11,000 F as children benefit from the 'social security'. It makes a total of about 37,000 (*Jacki*, please convert in marks.) With that, we can live well. The money for a sewing machine is ready, just the occasion was missing so far."

In a margin note, you add: "*Rémy*'s work is not intended for lasting. We are in contact with several people about an

---

[19] The Paris Subway.

'intelligence work'." This, however, is not what will occur, at least not before many years.

Anyway, this is the situation. Strictly speaking, I will not have been an educator's child longer than three weeks. However, we shall remain in a former children's home belonging to the UJRE, apparently without paying any rent, since you mention neither rent nor contract and will later write that with two little children "they cannot kick us out."

Meanwhile, Christmas is approaching. In order to take some vitamin C, the whole family is having some lemon juice with a spoon, the newborn included; and he likes it. I understand now why I still like this kind of flavor and do not reject acidic food.

During the holiday season, your brothers- and sisters-in-law will come to share your feasts: "We shall slurp some oysters, to my horror. All my viscera are turning around." How well I do understand you! How can anybody eat such disgusting things?

In the interval, *Onkel Jacki* has gone to winter sports. You say you are doing fine. Well, well, then enjoy! On Monday, January 7, 1952, you thank your parents for the various Christmas gifts. How often during these few years there will be talk of sending and receiving parcels!

Two months old, I open my eyes wide, make a few sounds and sleep well. You describe me as "an athlete" with some medium-blond hair and "brown-grey-yellow-green" eyes.

Cracked vertebra

In your letter dated Friday, February 8, 1952, the streak of bad luck has begun. In order not to startle your parents and brother, you start with small matters before you come out with telling that since Tuesday, February 5, you have been lying in hospital with a slightly cracked vertebra. You go into great detail on medical aspects, sketching your vertebra, and on the active support you have got from *Aniouta*, Lotte's daughter, now a hospital physician, without evoking the circumstances of your 'mishap.'

And here resides, for me, the first one of the mysteries around you. It seems clear that you fell out of our home's window. But how did it happen? Still a child, I once was scolded as I leaned too far out of a window. *Catia* took me mysteriously aside and revealed she had understood that *Maman Grète* had fallen out while cleaning windows. Was this an 'official statement' that was made to her when she asked why you were not there anymore? She added that afterwards you had to wear a plaster corset, which really happened and lasted until July.

Later, in a letter dated July 11, you will evoke your parents' confusion upon your telling 'the truth.' Well, which 'truth' was it? In Lotte's letter to your mother dated April 21, 1952, she blames your lack of rest after my birth, causing a tough winter time. She adds that, when you are not doing well, you do not complain but make yourself "the most unreasonable reproaches."

During your first weeks in plaster, you had been very depressed and anxious. What conclusions to draw from all this? That you had been physically so weary that a dizzy spell made you tilt off the window? That you had been so depressed that you wanted to end your life with a jump from the window? But you are far from stupid and know well that from the first upper floor one does hardly have any chances to die, but every chance to remain a cripple and be in amounts of pain.

I met once Zette, Pierre Lunet's widow, as well as Rosette, one of 'the tall' children, sent by Pierre from the *Coteaux* home to the *Plateau*, in order to take care of *Catia* and me during your transport to the hospital. Both of them have no doubt that it was a suicide. I am wondering. Perhaps they confuse this drama with the next one, which will cost your life one year later?

Rémy, my father, never wanted to enlighten us. This was related to the feeling of shame, to the pain, to what he had chosen to forget, after having switched to another life. If we had been able to speak freely about it, it would have done much good to us, *Catia* and me. Oh well, that is the way it is.

Anyway, we were placed in the care of a certain *Madame Hélène* who ran a kind of private baby care center in a house diagonally opposite the 18 *Allée du Plateau*. You report she provides a good care and *Catia* likes to go to her place.

From this time on, therefore, we have not much seen each other, *Maman Grète*; your absence already has begun for me since I have been placed—so to speak—in the hands of a second mother. In the beginning, you stay at Lotte's home in the *Rue Rollin*, in convalescence. Only *Catia* is old enough to be picked up on some Sundays by *Rémy* from Le Raincy to visit you.

Latin Quarter, April 1952: Grète with plaster-hiding gown blouse and Rémy *take* Catia *to the sandbox*

A photograph shows the three of you on stroll in the Latin Quarter. You wear the gown blouse you made yourself to hide your plaster corset.

You miss your children. On Saturday, March 15, exceptionally, a friend took me for a few hours to your place. I am "a very beautiful baby, round and well-groomed, and alert." Then you add: "He is becoming like his father, with brown eyes." You are glad you stopped my breast-feeding quite early: "Well, it was lucky indeed that he drinks from the bottle." Given the circumstances, it was a good thing, after all.

You had been "for a while unfortunately not quite at [your] best," had to sleep much, and wrote little. Lotte writes you should for the first time spend a fortnight in summer somewhere alone with your husband. This would be your first real vacation. And in future each unnecessary effort should be avoided. You also beg your parents for some financial support to make your everyday life easier, which you eventually will receive.

During your stay in *Rue Rollin*, *Rémy* is also living there and having lunch with you. He cycles to work, as you say, on a "bicycle with outboard motor." In Germany at that time, nobody knows what a *Vélo-Solex* is, this kind of bicycle with a small two-stroke engine before the handlebars and friction drive over the front tire. Many years later, in my last high-school years and as a college student, I too shall have such a vehicle, a brand new one as a gift from my father.

Without the burden of children, you recover well. Without any household efforts, too. You already evoked your need for a domestic help. Well then, your fall out of the window, was it perhaps a 'Freudian slip' to escape your daily efforts? Your spine, you write, does not cause you any pain.

Grète and Micha, *le Raincy, spring 1952*

On Wednesday, April 2, 1952, you write that you have seen me again, that I can sit and am laughing all the time. You long to return to Le Raincy but Lotte advises you against it; she thinks it would overstrain you. Moreover, you would not be capable of stooping, nor of carrying heavy weights. You confess that your new life and *Rémy's* new work have disoriented you to some extent. You would have been pleased to tailor garments with your new Singer sewing machine.

Otherwise, *Rémy* is "optimistic and active." On May 6, your plaster just has been cut on one side, so that you can take it off temporarily, such as for sleeping. On the twelveth, you report that you stay in Le Raincy during the weekends, where our apartment has been refurbished and enlarged after "the youth" who was sharing the first upper floor with us had gone away. *Catia* is surprised: "*Mama, you are wearing a wall!*"

My presence, too, sometimes. During the week, you still live in *Rue Rollin* to reproduce on Lotte's command an old-

Egyptian ship model after an original displayed at the Louvre Museum, originating from a Middle-Kingdom tomb, as I know now.

Why is there no letter between May 21 and June 11, 1952? Because your *Mutti* is there with us. I keep some photographs of this visit. Showing me, a nearly bald, big-headed infant in your arms or in Annette's, whom my uncle David recently married. And with *Catia*, now a pretty little girl aged almost three years.

In the meantime, your brother has written. He plans a big tour across France and Italy this summer, with three friends in a rented Volkswagen 'Beetle.' They would like to camp in our garden. This will occur, as shown by some other photographs: a couple of tents in the garden of Le Raincy, your *Vati* and *Jacki* with three other young men.

In your letter dated Wednesday, July 2, 1952, apart from the fact that you are not allowed to ride a bicycle for one year, the second mishap of your unlucky spell occurs. In veiled terms, you write about a "stomach ache," which was cured twelve days before with help of a physician. Further, you write that you had to pay thirty-five thousand francs and that, in spite of France being a Catholic country, money makes everything possible.

What to conclude, if not that you became pregnant again, did not feel strong enough to take care of a third child (so, your 1948 plan failed), and that you chose to undergo— probably with *Aniouta*'s complicity—a clandestine abortion? You say everything went well and you feel better again, but what must one think of the physical and especially the psychical consequences of such an experience?

It is not a trifle to prevent a child from being born; moreover it is a double burden since you do not feel at your best. Your only comfort is to say it is "better than a new window story." It might be one more clue of a relation between your feeling that 'you cannot do anymore' and your February 'accident.' A psychoanalyst might perhaps elaborate a symbolic association between 'I do not feel up to it' and 'I throw myself down.' Well, perhaps I am going too far...

Back to normal life

July 1952 appears to be a happy period. The weather is hot; while our family man is at work, you often get some rest with *Catia* in the garden and sometimes I am there too, although still 'in full pension.' I am "more and more beautiful" and my lower teeth are coming out.

You insist on your pleasant mood "without depression," and on your sincerity. One can feel how concerned your parents are, and you in turn are worried by their worrying.

On July 21, your *Mutti* and *Vati* come to visit us in Le Raincy with their brand new Volkswagen. *Catia* was impatient: "When is next week?" *Rémy* and you spend almost two weeks in early August in a hotel in Granville, at the English Channel seaside: your honeymoon, so to speak. Afterwards, we spend a week all together in Le Raincy, and then your parents leave for Switzerland.

At last! A summer ending without a home move; this is what you write on Thursday, September 4. How pleasant! If Jacki wants to spend the holidays with us, he will find us much better furnished, with gas heating.

I am not anymore at my 'baby-care mother's' home, temporarily. You describe me as "a tender meatball with looking eyes and a giant appetite." At present time, it is a great comfort for me to feel your tender love of yesterday. But back to the past: I am crawling on hands and feet, grasping a book shelve to stand up. I am still drinking out of the bottle. *Catia* has included me into her life.

No further letter before Friday, October 3. You make more compliments about your home, describing it as full of luxury. *Catia* had her third birthday. I am a "heavy boy," with seven teeth, among which three upper ones and my saliva running 'in streams.' "His merry and peaceful nature makes him laugh again and again in spite of his pain outbursts," this is what you say about me. A positive judgment. I can already say *"papa," "mama," "tsatsa"* (meaning *Catia*), and *"tatze"* (meaning *Katze*, 'cat' in German).

Which brings three remarks of mine: first, with hardly eleven months I am no late speaker; second, cats seem to have played an early role in my life—placed on the same level as family members—; and third, I am bilingual from start, because from the beginning you have been speaking German to me.

Your dream of a household help has become true. A certain Annie comes every forenoon and has lunch with us. For your wellness, it is fundamental. On October 22, you say you are supplemented in calcium, because of your many "tooth holes" (tooth decay).

I am starring once more. I have "conquered [my] father's heart in a storming assault," because I shout *"Papa!"* with a bright face when he comes home. Later in my life, it will be much more problematic for me to use this word. I also say *"hasser"* (for *Wasser*, water) when I mean the boiler and when I mean myself I say *"heesha."* I am "tall [?!] and fat," "very dexterous," "very affectionate." *Catia*, you say, is a little more complicated, but gentle and easy to handle. On November 6, having just become one year old, I make great efforts trying to speak and to walk. I say *büffel* for *Apfel* (apple). I stand up by grasping your clothes and I say: "Allez, allez! marcher!" (Come on, come on! walk!). My first sentence, perhaps?

You have visited the bone doctor. Your recovery is perfect, riding a bicycle no longer forbidden. You "had been fat" because of "a gland problem" but the case was solved with tablets. A hormone problem? Unfortunately, no household help anymore. Pregnant and abandoned, she is ashamed and dare not come anymore. You try to find a successor for her.

As a test, *Catia* goes to the public kindergarten. If she does not like it, you will bring her back to *Maman Hélène*.

Rémy now has in charge the lead of the local Livry-Gargan branch of the Movement for Peace, which occupies him three evenings a week, while you for your part give a weekly German lesson.

On Tuesday, November 18, you report that we are living merrily and that I am becoming "a little joker" (here indeed I recognize myself). *Catia* has provided me with the nicknames "*Rikiki*" or "Picasso."

Our family man is preparing the Vienna Congress for Peace, and that takes up a large part of his free time. You say that you do not get along too badly "with ups and downs of [your] nerves." An allusion to your 'bipolar' troubles.

On Wednesday, December 10, thirteen months old, I achieved three footsteps without holding, and I am very proud of it. I am running around with the broom, doing lots of damage. I shout *"nae, nae"*[20] when it is snowing. For my birthday, I have received a fur fabric cat as gift, of which my sister is jealous. I had a cold with a single-day fever (the first one in a long series).

At last! You have a new household help, *Madame Daix*. On the eighteenth, you report that I nibbled on some chocolate (same remark as for catching colds with fever). I made six steps without holding (hurray!).

Your brother *Jacki* has spent the holidays with us. All was well, excellent mood. I: *"ahki, ahki"* and to my teddy bear: *"bae, bae."* For my whole life I shall be strongly attached to my maternal uncle. He becomes like a second father to me and I am like the son he never had because he remained single. Still today, I keep using his favorite expressions, in German or translated into French.

Catastrophe on Thursday, January 29, 1953: household help gone. *Madame Daix*, who is a skilled nurse, was requisitioned for hospital work because of a lack of personnel caused by an influenza epidemic. She will have no successor. From now on, you will have to do all household chores with your own strength.

Rémy is becoming the manager of a servicing team instead of repairing devices himself at the customers' homes, in replacement for his former superior called up to the army. He will not be tipped anymore but in return get higher wages and more regular working times.

Your doctor prescribes extended biological tests, particu-

---

[20] Comes from the German word for 'snow:' *Schnee*.

larly concerning your thyroid. He would like to find the cause of your depressions. This time, you say, the winter passed without any depressions but it would be better to prevent the next one. From your lips to God's ear!

The weather is mild. You make plans for the summer vacation. You too wish to have a bicycle with a motor, otherwise you feel in Le Raincy "like in a cage." You wish to stroll along the banks of the Marne. Your parents are announced for Easter. You are worried. They now sleep in separate rooms, where can you accommodate them? One with us, the other at a hotel? How will the visit be, the atmosphere?

I run around in the garden and say *"Bonsoir, Papa"* (Good evening, Daddy). My eighth tooth causes problems, the next ones too. (Now I know why: I inherited your small mouth and *Papa*'s large teeth, which now are overlapping, and my wisdom teeth never have been able to come out.)

You "do not feel like" (do not have the strength?) searching for a new household help. You will again pass on your children to their 'foster mother,' even at night if necessary. On Wednesday, February 18, you ask *Mutti*, who recently has been on a rest-cure, if she is not too anxious before an Easter visit to our place in Le Raincy.

You too are in a kind of rest-cure. For a week, you have handed over us children to *Madame Hélène*, before "you are not able anymore," while *Catia* comes to visit you every day. You announce your goals: take another household help, acquire a motorized bicycle as soon as it gets warmer. You thank your parents for the promised financing of your vehicle.

You say I shall surprise my grandparents, whereas *Catia* did not change much. I am now a "heavy Siegfried" who still has not got his eighth tooth. At night, I wake up and call all persons whose names I know. I know but a few German words, however they are well 'anchored' and I am—already—able to translate: *"Der Besen, le balai."*[21]

---

[21] 'The broom' in German, French.

The end

Your last two letters are both dated Monday, March 16, 1953. One is to your *Mutti*; the other to your *Vati*, in a parliament session in Bonn, with similar content, but summed up. Your sleeping cure is lasting longer than you thought. Therefore, you left us with our 'foster mother.' We children are in good health. By using our room, your parents can sleep separate, without the need of a hotel. You make plans for transforming our home, since the inhabitants of the second upper floor do not need our bathing room anymore. You regret not being able to write to your relatives in Germany more often, but you think very much of them.

Well, that is all. Afterwards, I have nothing more written by you; I must reconstruct the end of your story with the elements I possess. My documents comprise your death record and a few letters from other persons.

The former is short: on (Monday,) March 23, 1953, (aged twenty-nine) you died at half past two in the afternoon in Montfermeil, 10 *Rue du Général-Leclerc* (address of the public hospital), recorded at four o'clock on the same day, according to the statement of Marcel Girard, employee (of the hospital?), residing in Montfermeil, 128 *Avenue des Myosotis*, by Adolphe Argence, Mayor of Montfermeil.

I keep a letter written by Lotte to your parents, dated April 10, confirming that the children are in good health and informing that *Catia* said: "Mama is very sick; On Sunday, she was sleeping all the time without playing with me." Lotte took *Rémy* for a couple of days to Normandy to provide him with some distraction. Not a single detail about your death.

Mutti has collected newspaper clips about suicide. She has received a letter from the neurologist, whose patient you had been in 1941 in Berlin, who reminds that, in the case of a "manic-depressive" disease like you had, nothing can be done. With this type of patients, a short-circuit action can occur at any time. Your parents should take comfort; nobody should feel any guilt (easy to say!).

Another source: my own more or less clear recollections of the more or less precise answers of my relatives and educators (*Rémy* primarily) to my and *Catia*'s questions.

Here are the elements I can draw out of all this. On Sunday, March 22, 1953, you took an overdose of medications used in your sleep-cure. *Rémy* came home at the end of the day and found you unconscious. You have left no last letter, so that no one can know if you wanted to put an end to your life or just be sure to sleep it off just once. My father always refused to adopt a position on it. For other persons, there is no doubt that it was suicide.

I tried hard to investigate. I wrote to the Montfermeil Hospital manager, requesting access to your patient file. His answer: no sign of your file in the archive because you had not been a regular hospital patient, neither admitted into a room, nor been in surgery. Too bad. If I had been able to know which dose of which substance did cost your life, whether or not you regained consciousness before passing away, then perhaps I might have had an explanation.

And, regarding the causes, in addition to all that I already said above, *Mutti* told me once that in her opinion *Rémy,* in the last period, had not been standing enough at your side. That he often would have stayed in *Rue Rollin.* Did he perhaps underestimate the seriousness of your state and therefore not done all that would have been necessary for your support? Incidentally, did you not also want to spare him?

So what? Accident or suicide? And why? These questions never stopped drilling in my mind. Now I know that I have to abandon this useless quest, and with it every hope for certainty. So it is and so it will remain, forever.

That is the reason why I had to write. To drop off all this and find some sort of peace, similar to resolving a conflict with somebody by writing the person a letter, even without sending it. I also always have experienced a vague feeling that I was guilty of having 'killed you,' but also of accusing you of having 'abandoned me.' I must try to calm down these feelings in me.

Epilogue

The further story will be carried out without you, *Maman Grète*. I shall make it short because after all I am not here to tell my own life. Am I? Well then, but not with as many details as for your life. One should not exaggerate. So, where did we stop? At the point when you still were *Mama* for me. Afterwards, I probably remained in the care of *Madame Hélène*, while *Catia* continued to go to the kindergarten.

The planned Easter visit was anticipated in utmost haste; your parents sleep at Lotte's in *Rue Rollin*, as documented in the already evoked letter from your former neurologist.

There have been no photographs made during this stay. I merely have a series of pictures dating from September showing my grandparents, my sister and me in Le Raincy. Each one of your parents is to be seen in separate images at your grave, in the new cemetery of Montfermeil.

It bears a temporary wooden sign with the inscription "GRETE STERMANN 1923 – 1953". A later photograph shows its final state: a concrete framing filled with pebbles and a concrete back panel with the same engraved text as above.

My father maintained no cemetery cult, maybe because his parents had been gassed and burned in Auschwitz, and his ancestors buried far away in Poland. Moreover, he had been constrained, as a Jewish forced laborer in the Camps, to destroy some Jewish tombstones.

A few years ago, I tried to find your tomb. At the Montfermeil town hall, I was given your grave file: a fifteen-year concession and a letter with a renewing proposal that came back without having reached its recipient. At that time, we already had moved twice. Your grave was given up and demolished by the municipality, your remains transferred into a common pit. You are dead, buried, abandoned and forgotten.

Your *Vati* became my *Opa*. This pet name had become available after your *Opa Adam* had passed away in 1929. In contrast, your *Mutti* also became my *Mutti*, just like your *Oma* also was mine. As an adult, she once told me that she had then said to me: "You have no *Mama* anymore, now I am your *Mutti*." To give *Rémy* some relief, my grandparents temporarily took me to their place in Hamburg. I was there alone from January to April 1954, as well as from November 1954 to April 1955.

Micha *in Hambourg, early 1955*

Catia joined me afterwards during the Easter vacation. I was barely three at that time; however, some images of the *Heymannstrasse* and of Hamburg in general have remained in my mind: the mail tossed onto the corridor floor through a slot in the apartment door; the elevated-train-line bridge at the end of the stree; the garbage-collecting trucks not with a wide opening in the back like in France but with a tilting elevator for the bins; a frozen canal with ice-skating boys; a bridge over railroad tracks with a cloud of steam suddenly wrapping me, accompanied by its humid coal smell; emergency accommodations in military sheet-metal half-cylinders, restless harbor water with a wheel steamer on which we are standing as a compact crowd; the painful sting of a vaccine in a doctor's office.

We also would travel to Kiel. As a very early and blurry image, the street leading to *Oma*'s garden, crossed in company of *Onkel Hans*, remains in my memory: my one and only Kiel recollection of that period.

There happens a strange generation slip; *Catia* and I take your place, so to speak. Incidentally, some former toys of *Jacki's* and your's are set at our disposal. In *Opa's* and *Mutti's* minds, there must have occurred, if not a confusion, at least a feeling of *déjà vu*. The older sister and younger brother repeat the situation of your family around 1929-1930.

Oma and *Mutti* are the only ones among my two grandmothers and four great-grandmothers I have known. No wonder that I feel much more attracted by my maternal, my German family branch than my paternal, my Polish one.

Catia *and* Micha *in Cochem on the Moselle, May 1955*

After Easter 1955, our grandparents drive us home by car via Bonn and along the Moselle River, as witnessed by some photographs.

Upon each trip from one country to the other, I have to re-learn French, while gradually forgetting German; and the other way around. This adaption phase will be shorter each time, until eventually I master both languages and the translation from one into the other.

Upheaval in our lives: *Rémy* has found a new companion and moved our home closer to his working place. We do not return to Le Raincy, but to the 11th Paris district, 57 *Rue de Charonne*, in a small attic apartment on the sixth upper floor, where *Rémy* and… Magali, his future second wife, await us. She was born in 1929 in Provence and is an acquaintance of Lotte. After you, Hélène and *Mutti*, she is my fourth mother, the one which will take care of me for the longest time.

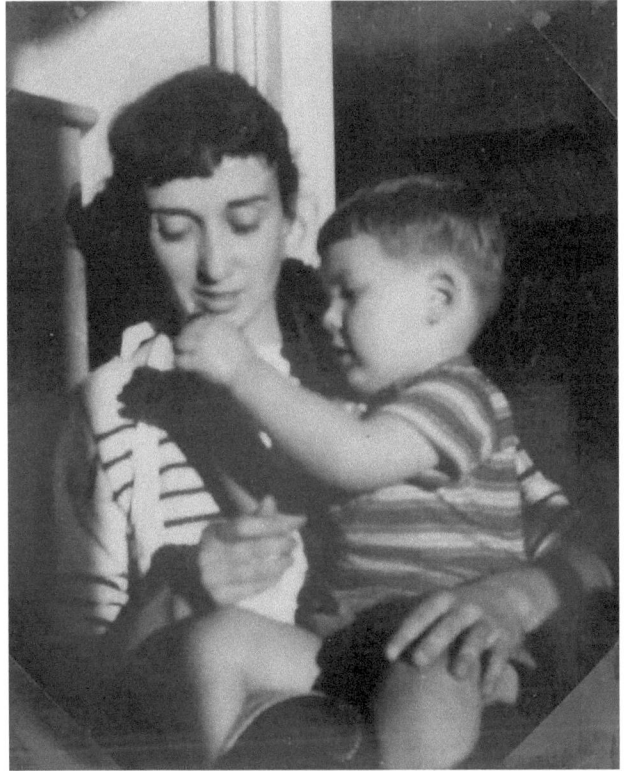

Magali and Micha, *May 1955*

In the following summer, making use of a compensation for the furniture, books, income and so on confiscated by the Hitler regime (I have received from the Hamburg State Archive the 125-page compensation file), your parents acquired a property in Mönkeberg on the Kiel East bank, which is near their birth place, in order to build on it their own single-family detached home.

The house in Mönkeberg in 1956

From the next year on, this will be the location of nearly all my vacations, partly with *Catia*, partly with Gilles, my half-brother, otherwise alone until the end of my college study period.

Catia *and* Micha *in Mönkeberg in 1956*

In 2006, after *Jacki*'s death, I am his sole heir, however I have to sell this property—with tearful eyes—due to lack of financial resources for its maintenance caused by a sinister case of money misappropriation by a household help. This dear house, poorly maintained, out of which I rescued as many archive items as I could, has been demolished and replaced with a couple of other homes. It will never have been inhabited by any other family than ours.

Catia will have a short and upset life. Strongly disturbed by your loss and its consequences, she will never admit the presence of Magali in the deepest of her heart, and she has been angry with *Rémy* because of his attitude. She has adopted a position of revolt, to be dismissed from school in eighth grade in order to fulfill her plans for becoming an actress.

Many wild, dramatic scenes took place in relation with it, in which she turned furious and our father called her 'mad like your mother.' Can you hear, *Maman Grète*, what he dared to do to your memory? Through your daughter, you have been called 'insane,' suffering from an allegedly inherited disease that all women since many generations supposedly were affected by. Whereas *Mutti*, on her part, believed in madness inherited from your paternal side.

Eternal problem of innate versus acquired. I rather tend to think that, on a possibly favoring ground, the influence of what was experienced is fundamental. When there really is a transmission, then like in the laundry where one color can stain from one item to another. In my sister's case, I do not think at all that the transformation of a merry, friendly, benevolent little girl into a wild cat (which, fortunately, she was not every day) can be a pure result of DNA combinations.

If, for my part, I escaped the worse, if I managed to marry, to have a son, to pursue a professional career till my retirement, then probably because the worst part happened over my head. I have indeed a good nature, I have for sure played the part of the 'good guy,' so I would not get into trouble, but the most important is that I did not have enough time and opportunities for building a sufficiently strong, tight and confiding relationship with you, *Maman Grète*, to suffer as much as *Catia* after we became the foster children of *Maman Magali*.

Catherine Stermann, photograph by André Nisak

So, *Catia* will achieve her goal because she started very early an actor's career, composing and singing songs in parallel, with her own guitar accompaniment.

However, her emotional condition will be worse from year to year. Her internal evil spirits will eventually push her to have all-round falling-outs within her professional milieu. After a first failed suicide, she takes her own life aged thirty-five years on April 11, 1985, using a cocktail of sleeping pills and alcohol.

For her not being forgotten, I have written articles about her in the French and German editions of Wikipedia, the online encyclopedia.

She and I shared the same questioning about you, *Maman Grète*. By joining you with similar means, did she perhaps want to make a definitive end with uncertainties?

Anyway, she managed to give me the deepest grief I had so far in my life. I never had such a collapse as in the days after. Did we not live together some beautiful and long moments of mutual understanding?

Wordplays

At this point of the original edition in French there is an extended intermediate chapter about wordplays. But because they are basically untranslatable I shall here only restitute a small part of it.

I wondered in my original book that I had written so much so far without including any pun or other play on words, which was, at second sight, not completely true.

Naturally, it was connected with the gloomy and oppressive aspects of my narrative. But now, to take a break—like at school—I feel like touching upon this funnier aspect of life.

I seem to be born in a family where playing with words has been everybody's practice. This might be the sign of a certain intellectual liveliness, handling languages not merely at face value but with a pinch of salt. I would like to give a few examples, after having remarked that—in my opinion—there are three fields in which wordplays are allowed, even awaited: psychoanalysis, poetry and advertising.

To look back a bit, I have heard from my uncle *Jacki* that *Oma* would call her son-in-law Wilhelm Grotkopp, husband of my grand-aunt *Emmi* using a nickname. To distinguish among several Willis in the family, she called him "*Onkel Willi mit der Brilli.*" The normal German form of 'wearing glasses' would have been *mit der Brille*. But changing the final 'e' for an 'i' makes a very funny rhyme in German ears.

The reader might remember my father, *Rémy*, having great fun with transfigured German idioms in the first days of his marriage (see "Rejected" Chapter, first paragraph). I heard from his lips a very funny joke when he had some German-speaking guests. When he was to invite his guests to take place around an abundant table, instead of the expected '*Bitte nehmen Sie Platz*' (please have seats), he would say: '*Bitte platzen Sie*' (please burst). Exploding laughter for this unexpected idiom was his inevitable reward.

My own wordplays are countless, but unfortunately mainly in French and some in German. I also improvised some in other languages such as Italian, Spanish, and English. But unfortunately I forgot the funniest ones. Here are the only ones I could say off the top of my head. When I get some ice cream from an English-speaking person, I usually say: 'Oh, what a nice cream!' During my stay in a British family in July 1971, I frequently was taken to some sightseeing by one of the sons who often had to stop at a shop to buy a pack of tissues because his nose suddenly was bleeding. When he came out of the shop, I would say to him: 'You and your bloody nose!'

And here I shall close this chapter and with it the first main part of this book.

PORTRAITS OF MATERNAL RELATIVES

Jacki

I already have told many things about your younger brother, *Maman Grète*. Knowing this, I shall try to avoid repeating myself too much while drawing his portrait.

He came into this world in Kiel on Thursday, March 12, 1925 as Jack Meitmann, like you without a middle name. Like yours, his Anglo-Saxon-like first name has a rather ambiguous history, making it similarly heavy to bear. Your father, in his childhood, used to play 'cowboys and Indians' in a boy's gang. Considering his broad and short hands, he had been given the 'Indian' pseudonym *Jack die Bärenklaue* (Bear-Paw Jack). For all his life, his friends, particularly in politics, will have called my grandfather *Jack*.

For my uncle, it will be hard to live as 'the son of...' and additionally bear the name everybody calls his father by. Indeed, in the family circle and among his close friends, his pet name *Jacki* will make the difference; however, much confusion will occur. It seems to me that he will endeavor for his whole life to be 'somebody' by himself.

His start in life runs parallel to yours, *Maman Grète*; therefore: see above. When comes the time of labor service, he becomes a smith at a Hamburg shipyard. Only your father is banned on residence, not the rest of the family. *Jacki*'s choice reminds of the original profession learnt by Hermann Adam, your maternal grandfather.

For his army conscription, he tries to enlist in the Navy Flak in order to avoid infantry and the East front. However, this will not be necessary because he will suffer from a heavy lung infection which will enable him to escape war service and to visit you in Jena for several periods.

After end of war, he studies political economy at Hamburg University. He is dreaming of achieving his study in a foreign country, if possible, in the United States. This will not happen, though, for reasons unknown to me.

In July 1949, with his diploma in his pocket, promoted by your *Vati*, who belongs to its supervisory board, he makes his debut with the GEG. This is the consumer cooperative close to the SPD. Herewith he reconnects with the activities of your maternal and paternal grandfathers, who had been founders of the Kiel Consumer Cooperative and the Kiel-Gaarden cooperative Bakery, respectively. But over time he becomes sick not only of the prevailing atmosphere, far away from the initially humanistic ideals of the cooperative, but also of still being regarded as his father's son.

In revolt against the bourgeois society, he moves to the workers' world, without neglecting your grandfathers' past.

In May or June 1952, he finds an employment as a welder on a Hamburg shipyard, different from the one where he did his labor service during the war. Merchant fleets are in full upbuilding. He participates in the construction of some large ships, among which the largest oil tanker of that time, the Onassis-owned *Al-Malik-Saud-Al-Awal*, a quite unusual ship's name he always remembered with pleasure and pride.

After your letters end, *Maman Grète*, I have no precise dating anymore. Therefore, I do not know after which interval *Jacki* eventually participates in founding a left-wing radical union section then in a large strike, and is dismissed on the ground of upraising the workers.

Jacki, Micha *and* Catia *in milk truck, 1958*

Making profit of his driving pleasure, he becomes then a delivery van driver, delivering supplies to shops in Hamburg subway stations, later a dairy truck driver in Lübeck, afterwards a bus driver for Lübeck workers commuting to a Hamburg shipyard (yet another one), a city bus driver between Lübeck and the seaside and finally a taxi driver in the same city.

After your *Vati* passes away in 1971, *Jacki* lives with *Mutti* in Mönkeberg and takes a professional training as a CoBOL programmer. His last position is with the large Hamburg Opel car dealer, in their computing department. He is a daily commuter from Mönkeberg to his working place, waking up very early. Strange career indeed for a graduate political economist!

Besides, he is passionately interested in the field of electoral reform. He develops a system with a numbering of the candidates—or candidate lists—by the voter in his order of preference. It is an improvement of the Australian system; it can grant for sure an absolute majority. He publishes two books, organizes discussion groups within the local SPD, especially with young people.

He also is a member of a society promoting the referendum on citizens' initiative called *Mehr Demokratie* (More Democracy). At the end of his life, as a single inhabitant of the Mönkeberg family house, he survives a stroke, is a heavily impaired walker and dies on Sunday, November 26, 2006 at *Klinik Preetz* Hospital from choking while eating (perhaps he fainted during his meal) a few days after successful surgery for a colon cancer.

He was a kind person with an accurate logic, lively curiosity, and well-established knowledge, always full of irony and humor. A civilized original who loved long conversations which he always made thrilling and enlightening. With him, I had a quasi father-and-son relationship. Even though in my opinion his emotional side was a little restrained, he constantly remained a model for me.

When I chose to start a career in information technology, it was through him I had understood this field might suit and please me, even without a degree in mathematical studies as was required in those days. So, I can say that his influence has—so to speak—guided me to the transverse paths I have walked in my life.

Mutti

Your and *Jacki*'s *Mutti*, who also—as I said—became mine and *Catia*'s, arrived on this planet—to speak like in *The Little Prince* by Antoine de Saint-Exupéry—on Saturday, January 11, 1902, at 2 p.m., in Kiel-Gaarden, in her parents' apartment located *Annenstrasse* 56, bearing the names Elsa Anna Adam (known as *Else*).

Her civil registration birth record is established after the statement of her father Karl Hermann Adam (bald, with moustache, roundish body, somewhat like Oliver Hardy), managing director, aged thirty-four years.

Her mother is Anna Pauline, née Feist, twenty-six years old. The two of them were born in farming and handcraft families in the distant Lower Silesia, which will become, after 1945, southwestern Poland. He was from Putschlau (now *Pęcław*), in the District of Glogau (*Głogów*), she from

Nimptsch (*Niemcza*) in the district of Breslau (*Wrocław*).

In Kiel, they have found each other as two 'emigrated' fellow compatriots in a 'foreign' city which had attracted them and Anna's brothers because of the many employment possibilities offered by the fast naval and industrial expansion initiated by the Emperor. Above all, it is the shipyards which need many working hands.

For Hermann, a skilled blacksmith, one of twelve siblings, there are here far better perspectives than in the poorer Silesian countryside, where only the eldest will inherit the farm, on which his family then only can live if he also operates some kind of craft.

Mutti was convinced she had read somewhere that the location name Gaarden came from the gardens of the former castle in which the future Czarina Kathrin II ('The Great') had passed a part of her childhood. But thanks to my own research I now know it better. The name comes from quite ordinary small fenced properties. In Kiel Castle was born and raised not Kathrin but her future husband, the later Czar Peter III, whereas she came from Stettin. This might have caused my grandmother's confusion.

Anyway, from the late 1800s, Gaarden is the location of the main Kiel shipyards and has become a working class suburb, administratively included in the main city in 1901.

Hermann Adam has generous, philanthropic ideals. He joins the SPD Party, in those days a socialist organization. To help his fellow workers bolster up their situations, he participates in union and strike activities. Consequently, he is dismissed from the shipyard. Never giving up, he founds on October 26, 1899, the Kiel Consumer Cooperative, among the first ones in Germany, taking over its management and development.

Although not close to the (Protestant) religion, her parents have the little Else christened on February 9, 1902, probably out of pure tradition. She is their first child. Then, there will follow Emma Dorothea (*Emmi*) in 1903, Hans Hermann in 1907 (future nuclear physicist and manager of the Kiel Engineer School) and last Anni Marie in 1909.

Else is a calm and intelligent girl with a nice appearance. Without effort, she passes ground school termination, and then attends a professional school in the field of furniture making. Later on, she will get some further training as an interior architect.

She carefully attends in parallel the educational evenings and lectures at a young workers' culture center. She also participates in the workers' gymnastics club, a hidden Socialist youth organization. With all her activities, she gains a large and loyal circle of friends on lifetime.

From her fifteenth year in 1917 until the evacuation of civilians from Berlin in 1943, she keeps a personal diary. I saved this big bunch of books together with other treasures in 2007 from the family house in Mönkeberg, before the latter was sold and demolished. Because of her hasty, almost stenographic old-German script, they are not easy to decipher but they are an invaluable knowledge source about *Mutti* and all family events around her. Through them I have acquired a fully different picture of her than by personal knowledge. In addition, she kept a children's diary about your and *Jacki*'s start in life, as well as a "Logbook" recording your last pre-war vacation aboard your family sailing boat from the Havel near Berlin to Müritz Lake further north. The latter with photographs and own drawings.

Mutti's diaries begin with her first great love. Ernst Busch (1900–1980) is a Kiel worker's son, two years older, who also regularly visits the young workers culture center. Besides his work on a shipyard, he takes theater and singing classes, encouraged by his girlfriend.

Micha, Opa *and Ernst Busch on Laboe beach in 1958*

He already is fascinating thanks to his magnetic attractive power and his strong, melodious voice. He will become a famous singer and actor, a convinced Communist who will collaborate with Bertolt Brecht and Hanns Eisler, among others. Their relation is strong, filled with great love, but still decent. It will not go beyond a magic kiss she will long remember.

After several back-and-forth episodes between separation and reunion, Else eventually decides that this passionate nature needs a woman living an artist's life as he does. In spite of her few tries on a theater stage, she does not feel a vocation for it.

In 1918, the most striking local event is the Kiel navy insurrection, which will fan the German Revolution and finally overthrow the *Kaiser*. She mentions the upbuilding soldier and worker councils which rule the city for a while, and the streets blocked by barricades with shots fired on the rebels.

In the following years, the eleven-year-older Karl Meitmann (see next chapter), son of a colleague and comrade of Hermann, is a frequent visitor of the Adams' home. He asks for *Emmy*'s hand in marriage but later on gives preference to Else whom he also likes. Your future *Mutti* feels attracted by his energy, his extravagance, his seductive charm. Between them arises a savage, strong, almost insane love.

Leading to their marriage on November 22, 1922 in Kiel; Karl's father just died on the day before. A modern couple, which is indeed what they want to be, without any complexes. Else is an enlightened, educated woman who aims at equal rights with men. When their mad love comes to an end, after a couple of years, their 'honeymoon' fades away. They did anyway not promise each other fidelity. Each of them will have several lovers over time. But they never will separate, for their children's sake, and because she is financially not independent.

I already told what happened afterwards when I described your life, *Maman Grète*. I shall restrict myself to mentioning that, after Berlin was evacuated in 1943, your *Mutti* finds a shelter with her Bäsler paternal cousins in Klosterfelde, north of Berlin. From there, forced by the regime to labor service, she chooses an employment as a furniture designer with Soldan, a company building sceneries for the moving picture industry. Because of the heavy bomb attacks, their premises had been transferred from Berlin further north to Oranienburg.

Mutti lives nearby, as a boarder of fine people. She carries on exchanging post cards fitted with a "Sign of life" ink stamp, with her husband remaining in Berlin, as well as with you and, in some periods, *Jacki*, to and from Jena. However, when, around April 1945, the thundering front is approaching, she feels that the Hitler regime is about finishing and she decides to return to her mother's in Kiel.

In the midst of the general panic, she takes a bicycle and flings herself onto the roads with her meager luggage. She travels partly by herself, avoiding the Russian or Polish outposts, partly with a squad of fleeing German soldiers with whom she is allowed to travel on board of a truck, and who respect her, as she told me. Three weeks later, she reaches her destination and finds *Oma*, who had been bombed-out twice, in her temporary apartment. A letter from Hamburg, sent by the three of you, will reach her in Kiel and this is how the post-war time of your reunited family begins.

I have known Mutti particularly well in Mönkeberg. From Easter to June 1957, before entering primary school, I spent three months there alone, before *Catia* joined us for the summer vacation. *Opa* called in almost as a visitor, so busy kept him his parliamentary activity in Bonn and in his Hamburg constituency. But every time he stopped by he would not forget to bring me something nice to nibble or to play with. In short, I was basically with my grandmother alone.

Once a week, we would go to downtown Kiel by harbor passenger ferry. We would have lunch at a restaurant, often at *Migasta*[22] facing the central railroad station, serving only food based on milk. Inevitably, the smell of rice pudding with sweetened cinnamon brings me back to that period, also to the times when *Mutti* herself would cook some. Then, we went invariably to the bank where she drew some cash. Because *Mutti* was in charge of the family money. When *Opa* stayed in Mönkeberg, she would fit him with the necessary amount for running daily errands. I often went with him, by the way and he would proudly exhibit "his grandson from Paris." But this is more something for next chapter; let us get back to the subject.

Supplied with her weekly cash, my grandmother would go shopping with me in *Holstenstrasse*, one of the very first pedestrian streets in Germany. Afterwards, we would pay a visit to *Oma* in her retirement home called *Stadtkloster*[23] in *Harmsstrasse*, not far from the Justice court builings.

---

[22] Coming from *Milch-Gaststätte* (milk restaurant)
[23] literally: 'City Convent'

Oma *(on her 80th birthday) and* Mutti
near the Kiel Stadtkloster in Harmstrasse, 1955

I see her still before me, this rather strict old lady dressed in black, with her Silesian accent. I believe she liked me, but I was impressed by her. We had some afternoon drink and cake. Mother and daughter would have a conversation while I was looking out of the window. On the opposite side of the street, I saw children playing in a schoolyard. Being near the Baltic Sea, I also observed the many seagulls perched on the surrounding roofs, all facing the wind so that their feathers kept straight, as I had been told. And the fact that they were not at sea was announcing a gale.

I also remember to have been playing alone in the garden in Mönkeberg during *Mutti*'s sacred afternoon nap. To avoid waking her up, I was not allowed to make any noise near her window. I was feeling lonely, slightly melancholic, looking forward to *Opa*'s return or *Jacki*'s visit, from which I would get some entertainment. Over my head, the wind made the leaves whisper and the clouds pass hastily before the sun. This typical cold-front weather, with the whispering of leaves, always awakes the same feelings in me and brings me back to that garden in the spring of 1957.

Although I was seen fully as a family member, I did not quite feel as comfortable with *Mutti* as with *Rémy* und Magali. Not indeed that Else would have been a spiteful person, far from it, but she was rather strict on educational principles. I had to take care that my finger nails were clean, sit upright at table, with my forearms on the table rim and not otherwise, shake visitors' hands with a bow, not speak to them before they asked me, say no nasty words, help set the table, and so forth.

I was strictly forbidden to leave her property, and to take the harbor ferry unaccompanied until I had a swimming certificate. I would shrug: as if one could fall from the ferry into the water! Should I have to learn flying like a bird to be allowed to travel by airplane? When I would object that in Paris I was allowed to do this and that, she would always answer: "Other countries, other customs."

I also found her excessively fearful. Everything would appear dangerous to her. During the night, she would leave a lamp in the corridor on, to discourage burglars. We children used to say in mockery: "otherwise muggers would come." She was often in the position of a victim, sighed and seemed to ask: 'Why for Heaven's sake is this happening to me?'

On the other hand, she was generous. She always fed us well, took us to excursions, or to the beach, with a tea-time break at a restaurant or provisions out of a bag. She provided us with clothing, shoes, accessories, toys, which *Rémy* and Magali hardly could have afforded.

And then there also took place these dispute scenes in which *Mutti* whined and *Opa*, ranting, slammed the doors. For what reasons? Certainly only trifling ones. But there certainly was a heavy backlog of conflicts 'in the cabinets.' Only *Jacki*, when he would come from Lübeck to call at his parents' house, knew how to make peace, with much calm and diplomacy, but constantly taking sides in favor of his mother. How better I felt when he was there!

I already have evoked the heavy silence about you, *Maman Grète*. However, I keep a moving memory of what *Mutti* told me on one evening of 1970. Like so often, I had returned from a day on the harbor ferries with my captain and sailor friends. We had been on a special tour for bringing children in care of Kiel 'Worker's Welfare' to a summer camp at Falkenstein Beach. On that day there had been their summer *fête*.

Because for several months I had been learning to play the flute, on that occasion I had taken my instrument along with me and played a few tunes. When, after returning to Mönkeberg, I mentioned my public success, my grandmother told me I reminded her of her beloved Grete who was so artistically talented and always would have enjoyed being the focus point of a circle. And she confessed that my flute reminded her of your playing the violin.

These words have warmed my heart incredibly. As if all these years of silence and dull shame feelings had been dissolved. In my ears, it sounded like: 'I love you and I admire you as I loved and admired my daughter. She survives through you.' Then, I also understood that the violin I often had used as a musical toy had belonged not to her, as *Mutti* had asserted often, but to you, my *Maman*.

Widowed in February 1971, Else has to undergo very bad times. Depression crises have brought her to the Kiel Nerve Clinic, later to the Heiligenhafen psychiatric hospital. She was not capable anymore of living on her own in her house, far too fearful, broken down, in spite of *Jacki*'s presence who, indeed, had joined her home but had been away for long hours every day, commuting to Hamburg.

In the early eighties, she gets a room in the favorably-located and rather pleasant nursing home of the Kiel Red Cross. There, she lives in a certain material comfort, without any heavy physical diseases, receiving her son's daily visits, occasionally also mine, with my wife and son. She fades away during her sleep on February 17, 1995, on the same day as her husband, just twenty-four years later.

On all these years, we never lost contact, be it merely with a little card for birthdays and holidays. I keep them all.

Opa

As I said, *Maman Grète*—and this is not new to you—, your *Vati* is my *Opa*. A quite uncommon personality, as we shall see.

His start in life happens on Friday, March 20, 1891, at 4 p.m. in Gaarden, *Kieler Strasse* at his parents' home, as Carl Friedrich Hermann Meitmann. His first name—most probably after the 1909 spelling reform—will be spelled 'Karl,' even in official documents. Before 1901, Gaarden is not yet a part of Kiel but an independent community.

He is the fifth child of the thirty-three-year-old metal fitter Johannes Leopold Friedrich Meitmann (felt hat, thick moustache) and of his wife Louise Friederike Ernestine

Mathilde, née Klein, (very beautiful and slightly ironic eyes, upright bearing), twenty-six years of age.

Johannes Meitmann was born in Wolgast, West-Pomerania, near Usedom Island and the Peene Mouth. His last name might derive from *Mähmann*,[24] and therefore have an agricultural-professional origin. Other forms could be *Meutmann, Meumann*, etc.

His ancestors originated from Stralsund, indirectly via Anklam. They can be traced back up to a certain Gabriel Meitmann, fine fabric weaver and guild master in Stralsund, about the first half of the seventeenth century. I possess the scanned copy of a letter from his hand in which he defends himself in a court matter against the guild of tailors. Beautiful script, beautiful signature. There follow more weavers, building or navigating ship carpenters, ship officers. In some Wolgast related family lines, there are also glaziers, as well as fish smokers and fishmongers.

In the course of generations, many of them are guild masters, a workers' union activity, so to speak, already. Johannes seems to have come to Kiel by himself around 1880, leaving his only sister in Wolgast. But she too will make the move, later on, and her daughter will marry Johannes' eldest

---

[24] German for 'mower.'

son.

Whereas Johannes Meitmann's wife Louise had come from Mecklenburg with her parents and siblings. All of them were born in Ribnitz but they can be found in the 1867 Rostock census, already nearer to Kiel, so it was a two-stroke move. Louise has an elder sister and two younger brothers. Their father is a sailor, later on a ship carpenter at sea, as well as one of her brothers, *Onkel Adolf*, of whom it is said that he survived in an air pouch the capsizing of his ship. He and the whole family had settled in Gaarden and were well known to the Meitmann family.

Before Little Karl came into this world in March 1891, there already had been[25] Wilhelmine in 1883 (later married in Hamburg), Heinrich in 1885, Wilhelm (known as *Bill*) in 1886 and Anton in 1889. After Karl, still is to come Elsa (known as *Else*) in 1893 (who will emigrate in April 1914 with her husband Hans Gülck to Vancouver, British Columbia, later to the Los Angeles area in California). An impressive sibling array.

Too impressive, maybe? Might perhaps the many pregnancies have weakened Louise's health? Anyway, she passes away in 1898, when my *Opa* just had celebrated his seventh birthday. Having meanwhile become a foreman, his father marries in 1901 Johanne Meyer, a forty-two-year-old widowed seamstress from Greifswald, not far from Wolgast.

From this second union originate Luisa Maria, born in 1902 (known as *Lissi*, the later Kiel Municipal Counselor Lisa Hansen, whom I have known well; very kind) and fi-

---

[25] See Documents Section, #5.

nally Hans in 1909 (who in Rostock will become a police constable and perish in the Second World War). I shall come back to the three eldest brothers in next chapter because their story is worth telling.

After your death, *Maman Grète*, my situation must have reminded him of his own childhood. Since, as I did, the young Karl got a stepmother; but with ten years he is older than me at his father's re-marriage. He never told me which relationship he had with Johanne (before my genealogical research, even her name was unknown to me), because we were not to speak about you and the similarity would have been too evident. Too bad... well, drop it.

In the early twentieth century, the German Union still is rather recent, not more than one generation. Important local cultural differences still are remaining. In Schleswig-Holstein, like in Mecklenburg-West-Pomerania, the Lower German dialect still is widely spoken. The elementary school teachers still use it. As late as in my own post-war time, sailors, farmers and workmen would use what they call *Platt* or *Plattdüütsch*. This ancient regional language derives from one of the roots of English; therefore, many words and grammar elements are closer to it than to German. One should note that there is an area between Kiel and Schleswig named *Angeln*. Just a few examples to illustrate: 'Five pence' is said *Fief Penn* (*Fünf Pfennig* in German); a 'pot' is called *Pott* instead of *Topf*; the upper end of a ship's mast is designated as *Topp*.

My *Opa* would intermingle Upper and Lower German constantly; he used the local language with his old friends, to say poems and tell tales; he often would sing *Platt* songs.

On this way, the dialect fully naturally 'slipped into my ear,' so that probably I am one of the very few Parisians able to understand it, just by the way.

So, our Karl attends elementary school. The newly recomposed family has moved from a Kiel suburb to the next one: Ellerbeck is located immediately north of Gaarden and also—by the way—bears a *Plattdüütsch* name meaning 'alder brook.' The corresponding German name would be *Erlenbach*. The boys from Ellerbeck have formed a gang, rival of its counterpart from Gaarden. Playing and fighting ground is a lake at the border between both communities called *Tröndelsee*.

The kids are fed with Wild-West novels by Jack London, Fenimore Cooper and Karl May, their German emulator. They dream of living in the wilderness, build huts and provide themselves with warrior names. This is how Karl becomes known among them as *Jack die Bärenklaue* ('Bearpaw Jack') because of his broad hands, as he told me himself. His whole appearance, by the way, is short and stocky, even more than mine. For his whole lifetime, his friends will call him *Jack*. Apart from *Mutti*, who would say *Kuddel* to him, which is a local Hamburg pet name for 'Karl.' And he in return would call her... *Mutti*, just like his children and grandchildren.

Ten years before my other great-grandfather Hermann Adam, in 1889, the shipyard worker Johannes Meitmann showed him the way, so to speak, by founding the Gaarden Cooperative Bakery.

In 1905, with his elementary school certificate in his pocket, his son Karl starts an apprenticeship for trading and bookkeeping with a grain-wholesale company, later switching to a coal trade one. Simultaneously, he attends a school of Commerce in which he studies accounting and commercial law. In 1908, he becomes in parallel a gymnastics trainer in a socialist-driven youth organization, a cover for unauthorized political education.

His activity as a trading employee (bookkeeper) starts in 1909 with the GEG (large wholesale purchasing company for cooperatives) in Hamburg. Meanwhile, he carries on with his own education and the sports training of young workers in Hamburg.

That is where in 1912 he is caught up by military service. He, an internationalist and convinced pacifist! Not enough that he has to undergo a three-year training, ending as a corporal, even much worse: precisely then the First World War bursts out. Three wounds, nomination as a sergeant, Iron-Cross medal.

Passionately French-friendly like many Germans, he told me once how on one occasion he suddenly was facing a French soldier and how hard it was for him to shoot for saving his own life. I do not know how intense his anti-militarism had been before; at the latest then it had become so. He also had secretly fraternized with the French population, even helping out on a farm in absence of the family man who was at the fighting front, as he also told me.

Discharged home in December 1918, he becomes the secretary of the Deputy President of the Schleswig-Holstein Government in Schleswig. Duties of the Deputy: political monitoring and conversion of the Province administration to the new democratic-republican principles. Karl's particular mission: negotiating with administrative managers and offices about how to apply the instructions of the new government.

On the following year, he is the first secretary of the German plenipotentiary at the *International Commission Sleswig*, the inter-allied Supervision Commission for the mainly Danish-speaking North-Schleswig independence plebiscite. He is responsible for the organization and supervision of the German campaign in both zones of the plebiscite area. After the vote on March 24, 1920, the German-Danish border is redrawn further south and Flensburg reunited as a German city.

After the plebiscite is performed, Karl is acting in place of his boss Dr. Adolf Köster, who had been nominated as German Minister for Internal and International Affairs. His important accomplishments make him noticeable for his organization and persuasion skills. For going on, the best is to quote from his own resume I found in his post-Nazi reparation file:

> "1920 (March) - On behalf of the State Commissary commissioned by the State President for restoring peaceful and orderly conditions, I have performed autonomously and according to my own vision and knowledge the organization and leadership—also on military aspects—of the resistance of Government-loyal forces in order to repress the Kapp-Putsch in Schleswig-Holstein, while on several occasions I put my own life at risk with a weapon in my hand.
>
> After I had fulfilled this mission, I was desig-

nated by the Prussian Minister of Interior, whom I was directly and solely reporting to, as a political civil commissary for the Province of Schleswig-Holstein. Duties: setting up and securing the State Police in the spirit of the democratic legislation with veto right against every Police decision until personal decision after reporting to the Minister of Interior.

(...)

I have refused my proposed nomination as a Prussian State counselor by the Prussian Minister of Interior, so I could dedicate myself with my knowledge and experience to the liberal-democratic workers' movement. For the same reason, I have rejected a proposal for becoming the Kiel Police Superintendent."

To perform his various tasks, he had attended eight semesters at Kiel University in constitutional, administrative, and penal law, as well as law philosophy.

In 1924, Karl is founder of the *Reichsbanner Schwarz-Rot-Gold* for Schleswig-Holstein, para-military security forces of the SPD. The next steps of his career are in 1926 his election as Schleswig-Holstein District Secretary of the Social-Democratic Party, in 1928 as First President of the SPD regional organization in Hamburg and member of the party's executive committee, and finally in 1929 as a member of the Hamburg Regional Parliament the so-called *Bürgerschaft*.

Opa, *ca 1930*

In the meantime, as I said, he got married, had his both children, moved from Kiel to Altona, then to Hamburg-Fuhlsbüttel.

When the Hitler gang seizes power in 1933, he is arrested three times.[26] With help of his secretary, he burns many invaluable yet compromising papers in his laundry room. On his third arrest on June 16, 1933, during a semi-secret meeting of the Hamburg SPD management, he is taken into custody in the Fuhlsbüttel Concentration Camp, quite close to his home. Even under severe torture, he does not reveal who produced a document found by the *Gestapo*, with the goal of organizing the exile in Prague of the SPD management.

By cross-examining several sources, I was able to get a picture of the circumstances under which he was released in

---

[26] See "Banished" Chapter above for details.

late October 1933. His defender, the respected attorney Dr. Herbert Ruscheweyh, managed to prove his imprisonment was illegal and to emphasize that, during the Schleswig events in March 1920, Karl saved a titled officer from a murderous crowd by standing in between with a pistol in his hand. This must have instilled a certain consideration into these Nazis' minds since his imprisonment was changed into banishment.

I have described in the first part of this book how the Meitmann family went on. When the war was over, having gained back his functions, Karl became additionally a member of the *Bundestag*, the Parliament, for the first three legislatures after the Federal Republic of Germany was established in 1949. Additionally, he was a member of the party's executive committee.

On March 20, 1961, at his seventieth birthday, he resigns from all his responsibilities to enjoy his idle time at his Mönkeberg home. Every time he has to go to downtown Kiel, he drives through Ellerbeck and Gaarden, along the shipyards, reminding him of his history.

My oldest memory of my *Opa* naturally dates back to the time after your passing away, *Maman Grète*. I am on the rear seat of the Volkswagen, on our way to Germany. He turns around to me and says with a malicious-comical facial expression: "You are a *Pulcinella*." Because of his accent, I always thought he was saying *Putschineller* and that this was a word of his own. Only decades later, thanks to Stravinsky, I have understood that this was a character from the traditional Italian *Commedia dell'Arte*.

He was awfully fond of little children. He would make

me laugh, playing the clown. Every time he saw a child that was a walking beginner, he was in admiration.

His generosity was great; he always wanted to offer something: "Would you like an ice-cream?" was one of his most typical questions. But he could also offer something to drink, a treat, a toy, a ride on a merry-go-round and so on. In my eyes, he was like a beardless Santa-Claus.

There was constantly a song on his lips, be it only for inventing some new verses in relation with what we just were doing. He did not sing the tunes particularly cleanly, but with conviction. They were songs of all types, children's songs, seamen's songs in German or dialect, political songs, fighting songs, Communist and Spanish-War songs from the records sung by Ernst Busch.[27] He also often recited long poems by Goethe or Schiller.

Another memory: I see myself back in Mönkeberg, in the small room of the cellar that was his workshop, lying on a board under his workbench, watching him and listening to his explanations.

Affectionately, he would call me *mien Jung*,[28] like to *Catia* he would say *mien Deern*.[29] He played much with us and with Gilles all sorts of board and card games, as well as outdoor games, such as deck-tennis, badminton, or crocket. However, he spoiled all my taste for board games because his only pleasure consisted of winning loudly and triumphantly against me. He also would cheat at many games,

---

[27] See "*Mutti*" Chapter above, her youth love.
[28] "My boy," in *Plattdüütsch*
[29] "My girl."

just for winning.

To make us sleep, he would tell us stories, but would often start dozing himself while speaking. When he did not know anymore what to tell, then he would say: "Once upon a time, there was a man who had seven sons. The seven sons said 'Father, please tell us a story.' Then, the father began: Once upon a time, there was a man who had seven sons..." and so on, until we had more than enough.

He was indeed a special person, truly impregnated by love for wilderness life, with a bare body in open air and sun. He had a kind of ideal of the 'noble savage' in the sense of Jean-Jacques Rousseau.[30] He loved to be on the water, in the water and under water. His favorite prank was to jump from a diving board with his pipe smoking, to swim under water and reappear still smoking his pipe. Any trick? With his back turned to the audience, he quickly closed the mouthpiece with one finger while pressing the pipe bowl against his forearm, so he could swim almost normally. Reverse manipulation when his head reappeared, still not facing the audience, then turning back to it under cheering applause.

At the steering wheel, he was a scary driver, impatient, imprudent, rather confused with traffic regulations. I still can see *Mutti* on the front passenger seat taking a deep breath at every intersection, sometimes covering her face with her hands. In the worst cases there also came an *"Ach, Kuddel!"* exclamation.

---

[30] Swiss-French philosopher and writer (1712–1778) who was one of the inspirers of the French Revolution.

My *Opa* was a heavy smoker, whence chronic bronchitis causing coughing and spitting, also out of the car window when he was driving. On one occasion, he forgot that he had not opened the window pane.

Once retired, he spends his time mainly taking care of his boat, to escape conjugal cohabitation as often as possible. He had acquired a traditional fishermen's rowing boat, added a couple of short bamboo masts—he was very fond of this material—with old-style brown sails. His *Passat*[31] sailing boat with its tinkered sheet-metal fin keel maneuvered heavily. Its unreliable 10-HP Volvo-Penta gasoline engine caused endless telephone conversations in *Plattdüütsch* with a friend of his.

Mutti asserted that *Rémy* had expressly forbidden that his children set foot on *Opa*'s boat. Therefore, I never sailed with the *Passat*. But this did not prevent my grandfather from contaminating me with his love for shipping. He also infected me with his disliking the Navy.

A very pregnant memory is connected with the occasions when there were visitors at his home, when perhaps a beer or a brandy had been taken and a political debate would flare up. When my grandfather then would take the floor, in a loud, decided voice, with a hurrying flow, he would gain such a momentum that he became hard to stop.

My last scene with him takes place in his room at Kiel City Hospital in September 1970. As a consequence of his tobacco smoking and chronic bronchitis, he suffered from arteriosclerosis and a stomach ulcer. A dramatic gastric per-

---

[31] German word for 'Tradewind.'

foration had caused his transport to hospital in emergency.

During one of my last visits at his bedside, when he felt that we probably would never meet again, he in a certain sense made his farewell in that he firmly took me in his arms and spoke to me about you, *Maman Grète*. More precisely, about the tormenting feeling of guilt because he had not informed *Rémy* about your psychiatric past. He weeped and affirmed he could not have acted otherwise. If only he had known. He was awfully sorry but he had to say it to me, in order to relieve his conscience.

I was so deeply shaken that till late at night I had running tears. I think I never cried so much in my whole life: in the public transport, at home. I remained by myself, did not want to speak to anyone. I do not know what *Mutti* and *Jacki* thought of my behavior, I have forgotten whether or not I shared anything with them. Black-out. I only remember my overwhelming sorrow.

Why? I felt ashamed that I sometimes had mocked my old, somewhat run-down, hearing-impaired, ridiculous *Opa*. Now I was discovering how much sensitivity and suffering had been hidden in his soul, without me guessing it. His guilt feelings were contagious.

He never returned home afterwards. His stay in hospital lasted from September to February. He calmly went away in his sleep on Wednesday, February 17, 1971. He, who exemplified in my eyes old age, with his snow-white hair and rosacea complexion, missed his eightieth birthday by five weeks.

Adventure of the three Meitmann Brothers

Of the story that comes now not everything is known to me; far from it. There is what my *Opa* told me about it (or at least what remains of it in my memory). There are also the particulars transmitted to me by *Jacki* during my last visit to him, with my son in January 2004, which had the purpose of harvesting as much information about our family history as possible. Additionally, there are also data accessible via Internet and my contacts with the American descendents of one of the story 'heroes. '

First my childhood memories: Two brothers of my grandfather's, *Bill* and Anton Meitmann, had travelled to America, where they had experienced lots of adventures, causing much trouble. After returning to Kiel, they had become coastal fishermen, owning a wooden fishing boat moored close to Downtown Kiel. Expressed like this, it was already fabulous enough.

Bill

Anton

In the time from 1956 on when I would travel to Kiel, *Bill* already had passed away and Anton was retired. Too bad, I would have been so fond of steering a big fishing boat. Through *Jacki*, I learned in 2004 (or was reminded if I had forgotten it) that there had been a third man in the story, namely the oldest brother, Heinrich Meitmann. So, they had not travelled as a pair but as a trio.

And when I asked my uncle what had become of Heinrich, why he had not joined his brothers as a fisherman, he answered he did not know, nobody had spoken to him about Heinrich (let alone to me...), it was only the other two he had known well. About the oldest brother, he shrugged his shoulders and proposed: "disappeared in America."

Regarding the adventures experienced, he spoke of tramping across North America as stowaways aboard freight trains, of hanging around with all possible people, of doing all possible jobs and even of participating in the Mexican Revolution under Pancho Villa. *Bill* and Anton, *Jacki* said, came back with such a disgust of the American system, of its methods, of King Dollar, that, while they had departed as Socialists, they returned as Communists. They had become freelance fishermen in order not to be depending on a Capitalist boss.

Jacki also had good memories of his first cousin Wilhelm Meitmann, known as *Willimann*, Anton's son, a women seducer and *bon-vivant*, to whom his mother Amalie (known as *Male*) secretly had brought a bottle of wine into his hospital room while he was recovering from surgery.

Regarding his father, my granduncle Anton, it is said that during the sixties he had been found at a cigarette vending machine, obviously thinking it was a telephone booth, where he tried to speak to 'Comrade Thälmann,' the former Hamburg Communist leader murdered by the Nazis in the Buchenwald Concentration Camp.

And then the documents I came across. On the one side, I had a very interesting information exchange with a lady in the Kiel *Meldeamt*, the citizen's registration office, who provided me with a wealth of data about all my relatives having lived in town. On this way, I learned the names of the three wives *Willimann* had. With the second among them, he had a daughter, Carmen, who later emigrated with her mother to Great-Britain and was adopted by her stepfather as Cooper.

This information is part of my family research publicly stored on a specialized Internet site. One fine day in 2014, the Carmen in question surprised me with a contact request. She is your first cousin's daughter, *Maman Grète*, of whom I did not have the least hope ever to hear. She was quite happy to have found at last one relative with whom she could exchange about our common family history. We have been maintaining an interesting, regular, and hearty e-mail correspondence.

On the other side, there are information items on the World-Wide Web. I could find the most interesting ones on the Ellis Island Web site, where passenger lists of the emigrant ships arriving in New York can be retrieved. There, I found the three Meitmann brothers and could hardly believe my own eyes when I discovered all that had not been revealed to me before.

First the travel date: arrival in New York on May 6, 1915. Really? Right in the middle of the First World War? While Karl was squatting in the trenches, his three brothers had escaped! But how? The circumstances give us some clues. The ship, the *Hellig Olaf* (Saint Olaf) is flying the Danish flag and comes from Copenhagen. The three brothers are listed on three adjacent lines, as Meitmann *Vilhelm* (28, brewer), Heinrich (30, worker) and Anton (26, mason). Nationality: Denmark, Place of birth: Copenhagen.

Hell's bells! How could they, in the middle of the World War, get from Kiel to Copenhagen, and how could they have been considered by the Danish crew as Danes? By speaking their *Plattdüüütsch*? A few word roots indeed are similar but the pronunciation is completely different. No way! Only plausible explanation: benevolent protection. Danish fishing boats might have made them secretly cross the Baltic Sea. Perhaps they had a connection with Danish Socialists who could have provided them with the necessary means for their flight: forged passports and benevolent persons on board, among others. A prank played by the Danes against the German Empire, in a certain sense.

Poor Karl, who on his part had to remain for seven long years in the Imperial eagle's claws! I am convinced that he would have played the 'fourth musketeer' if he only had been able to do so. He never revealed it to me, but when he was informed of the prank, he certainly had envied his brothers.

Next surprise: their destination, crossed-out and re-written. Originally, they wanted to visit their brother-in-law Hans Gülck in Lynn (Valley), Vancouver, British Columbia, Canada. This made sense. But why replace this destination with name and address of a New York clergyman? Perhaps because during their crossing they had heard that Canada, belonging to the British Crown and therefore belligerent, had made all Germans present on their territory prisoners of war.

As a matter of fact, period letters reveal that Hans Gülck was imprisoned from mid-1915 until end of war in a camp in Vernon, British Columbia. And regarding our fellows, all three of them are stamped by the United States Authorities as "non immigrant" and "in transit." Then, I lose their scents and can only orient myself with the indications above.

Oh yes! One thing: The youngest Meitmann sister, Elsa, Hans Gülck's wife, was recorded on October 27, 1917, crossing the border, travelling without her husband but with her two-year-old son Carl from Lynn Valley, northern Vancouver, to Ontario, California (a suburb of Los Angeles), thousands of miles to the south. Destination of the long trip: she was joining her brother Heinrich, who was to take care of them during her husband's captivity. After the (first) war, the Gülck couple will settle definitively in the Los Angeles area.

Now, how about this Heinrich who supposedly "disappeared in America"? Well, here I have some other on-line sources (on the 'Mormon' Web site, among others), according to which, in addition to his oldest son Johannes, born in 1910 (so, in 1915 he had left wife and son in Kiel; Anton too was already married), he had also had a Heinrich Junior who, like you, *Maman Grète*, was born in Kiel in 1923, but soon must have died because there came another boy of the same name in 1926. Meaning that my granduncle Heinrich did indeed return to Kiel after 1918. Together with his brothers, or did he for a while "disappear in America" first? I do not know.

Anyway, he returned to the States in 1924–1925, and another time, definitively, on January 24, 1927. He was travelling to a friend in Kansas City. *Anni*, his wife and first cousin (born in Wolgast), followed him on the next seventh of November with both her sons (including the baby). Later on, the family settled in Seattle, Washington on the Pacific Coast, not so far after all from Vancouver.

And that is where I found them, in the Seattle area, in 2006. The said parents of course not; they had passed away in 1963 and 1974 respectively. But 'the baby' of 1926 was still alive, although bedridden. With one of her daughters who picked up the telephone I could have a conversation. Second cousins are we, like with Carmen from Great-Britain.

In last minute, so to speak, I could inform *Jacki* that I had found his first cousin in Seattle, Heinrich's son, when I had him on the telephone on the day before his surgery at Preetz Hospital. On the following Sunday, my beloved uncle died; it had been our last conversation.

Through my Seattle relatives, I have further heard that my granduncle Heinrich, like his brother Anton, ended his life in a psychiatric hospital, his son Johannes as well, who reportedly had taken his own life at the age of twenty-one years.

Oh! What a family you came from, *Maman*!

PORTRAITS OF PATERNAL RELATIVES

Rémy

Rémy *with his children, Easter 1954*

Act 2, scenery change. Let us forget Germany and your Lutheran-Protestant ancestors, *Maman Grète*. The roots of your husband are in Poland, in Jewish circles. He himself was born on March 7, 1923, at Rothschild Hospital in the 12th Disctrict of Paris, as Henry Stermann. He had been preceded in 1921 by his brother Camille. My father's birth record is a first-class genealogic curiosity. There is written, in the main text column:

> "On the seventh of March thousand nine hundred twenty-three at seven hours thirty minutes was

born, *Rue Santerre* 15, Henry, of male gender [son] of Leiser Stermann, born in Karkoff (Russia) in the year thousand eight hundred ninety six and of Rachel Popiolek, born in Karkoff (Russia) in the year thousand eight hundred ninety-eight, without occupation, his legitimate wife, both residing in Paris, *Rue des Jardins Saint-Paul* 31 (...)"

You wonder already, my dear reader: did I not say "roots in Poland"? Be reassured, your wondering still is far from ending. I go on. First margin mention:

"On the twenty-sixth of February thousand nine hundred thirty one, in the 15th District Townhall of Paris, recognizd by Leiser Stermann and Rachel Popiolek."

But why "recognized"? Was he not already designated as legitimate son of his both parents? Second margin mention:

"As a consequence of the marriage occurred on the seventeenth of March thousand nine hundred thirty-one between Leiser Stermann and Rachel Popiolek, declared a legitimate child."

But why declared legitimate after his parents' marriage? Was he not in the main text already a legitimate son of married parents? Honestly, how can a serious Civil Registration clerk ever write down such mentions without a court of justice correcting the original record? How careless!

Dear fellow genealogists, I warn you: Never trust records blindly. Can you imagine, *Maman*, that according to *Catia*'s death record you would have been still alive in 1985? Explanation: the declarant not always is informed right, that is he does not always have all rent documents at hand.

The good declaring hospital employee in 1923 could probably not imagine that a Jewish couple could have a child without being married. The Police commissioner who reported *Catia*'s death in absence of relatives during Easter vacation had no access to our parents' family book, and so on.

And what are the other curiosities in *Rémy*'s birth record? To make it short here, I shall tell separately in next chapter the story of my paternal grandparents, of the ones I have not known.

For the moment, *Rémy* still is Little Henry. He will be followed by Nathan in 1927, David in 1931 and Monique in 1936, the only girl among the five siblings. One can feel the parents' tendency to integration by the fact that they did not choose only typical Jewish given names for their children. Camille, Henry ('Henri' would have been even more typical) and Monique are in those years usual names for French children.

In the meantime, the family has moved into the already mentioned subsidized housing apartment of the Rothschild Foundation at 15 *Rue Bargue*, Paris 15. The family man works as a tailor contractor at home, reads the worker-friendly newspaper *Naïe Presse*. Henry attends the public elementary school and endeavors to be a little Parisian like the others, although he is somewhat ashamed of his parents who came from a foreign country, speak foreign languages (and hardly French) and live according to foreign customs.

Henry and Nathan

In the streets, he plays with boys from the neighborhood. Through the back door, without buying any tickets, they attend the nearby "lousy cinema" and watch all possible movies. They use one of their favorite ironic sentences "Have you seen *Ben Hur* in color?" when one of them is exaggeratedly proud of something.

At home, the parents speak Yiddish. When the children should not understand, then Polish. After finishing the elementary school, Henry does not—as far as I know—start an apprenticeship for a particular occupation. I do not know the reason why. He could have acquired gentlemen's tailor skills with his father, otherwise become factory worker like his elder brother. He never told me if he had a particular occupation in view, or perhaps I do not remember well.

I cannot well distinguish between his pre-war activities and the necessarily modest unofficial jobs he had to find during German Occupation, after Marshall Pétain's 'Jewish Laws' had imposed professional prohibition. By the way, the three brothers Camille, Henry, and Nathan, refused to wear the infamous yellow star.

It may have been during the war that he worked for the radio set repair workshop of *Monsieur Routier* whom I also have known later. It may have been before or during the war that he was an usher at the 'lousy cinema.' What I know for sure is that during the war he delivered boxes to customers.

After the parents had been arrested on July 16, 1942, in the framework of the notorious *Vel d'Hiv*[32] police mass-raid against non-French Jews, (the children are considered French and left alone in the apartment), Little Monique, five and a half years old, is taken in care by benevolent neighbors and hidden as a pretended Catholic child by some of their relatives in the French Alps.

The eleven-year-old David is sent by his *Rue Vigée-Lebrun* Elementary School manager (who will later be arrested and executed for having saved Jewish children) to a

---

[32] This was the popular nickname for the *Vélodrome d'hiver* (Winter Indoor Velodrome) in Paris 15, where thousands of families were detained for days before being abducted via the Camps at Drancy (near Paris), Pithiviers and Beaune-la-Rolande (near Orléans) to Auschwitz and mass-murdered.

summer camp in Central France. After the summer vacation is over, all Jewish pupils are secretly distributed among Communist farmers in the same area.

These families will foster for years both siblings for free and put their own lives at risk. My uncle and my aunt will successfully apply to the *Yad Vashem* Memorial so their protectors will be granted 'Righteous among Nations' distinctions.

Meanwhile, the three oldest, Camille, Henry and Nathan, must cope by themselves with the situation. They live in a small servant room at *Rue des Favorites*, with the goodwill of their illegal employers, among which perhaps the said *Monsieur Routier*.

It is more than probable that they were betrayed, because on June 17, 1944, early in the morning, a group of SS-men suddenly intrude into their refuge and arrest all three of them, aged at that time twenty-three, twenty-one and seventeen, respectively. They are abducted to the Concentration Camp of Drancy in the northern surroundings of Paris and there, without violence, they are questioned by the SS-man with the highest rank. After the war, my father will recognize this man on photographs. It is the commander of the camp, Alois Brunner, who is supposed to have been a secret refugee in Syria for many years under the protection of the local dictator.

One of my father's camp memories: he is standing near the barbed-wire camp fence and tries to get some information from a French *gendarme* guard. The man reacts immediately: "Beat it or I shoot at you!"

Upon their arrival at Drancy, they are registered under the numbers 23977 – 23979. In the camp register there is also a receipt for two hundred and seventy francs, which Camille had in his pocket and which were confiscated.[33]

The three brothers are packed into the freight-train Transport number 76, which departs on June 30, 1944 for an unknown destination, designated among the detainees as *Pitchipoi*. After four days in inhumane conditions, nightly arrival of the train at a platform lit by powerful spotlights. Incredible scramble, skinny people in pajamas, pulling handcarts. First reaction at this view: "What kind of a puppet show is that?"

The 'pajamas' help them step out. Selection. My father goes in the right file, the one that does not go straight to the gas chambers. So do his brothers. They are in Auschwitz-Birkenau. He asks around if anybody might have seen his parents. In place of an answer, someone points at one of the long chimneys, which spit out stinking black smoke.

Never will my father reveal what he felt when he understood why he would not see his parents again. He probably had no words for it. The repression (in the sense of Freud) did the rest.

The three brothers are placed in a marching column which walks to the Work Camp, Auschwitz III Monowitz, some six miles to the east. Here is in construction an industrial complex for producing artificial rubber under the Buna brand, an indispensable military production as part of the German self-sufficiency, the country being cut from the

---

[33] See Documents Section, #10 and #11.

sources to natural rubber, particularly for its vehicle tires. Plant owner is the trust named *Kombinat IG Farbenindustrie*, which the Nazis set together out of the main German chemical manufacturers Höchst, Bayer, BASF, among others.

When the war is over, these companies will become independent again and continue their activities unhindered. This industry makes its profit off the slaves provided by Heinrich Himmler's troops in the framework of the "final solution of the Jewish question." This is how 'work costs' are minimized by disregarding any human aspects. These gangsters do not even see in them full members of mankind.

After a two-month start period with the most wearing and humiliating tasks (such as destroying Jewish tombstones or digging unnecessary trenches), to break them down and make any resistance impossible, newcomers are assigned working positions within the plant. One of the prisoners had said to them in Yiddish that it was vital to declare a skilled profession. Henry makes the statement that he is an electrician. As the prisoner tattooed with the identification A16884 on his left forearm, he is provided with a useless but weather-protected occupation as an instrument checker.

On several occasions, the air-raid sirens blare. English-American bombers. All men to the air-raid shelters, except the prisoners who remain exposed to the bombs, and cheering in the factory yard. Unfortunately, the damages will not be sufficient to set them free.

This situation lasts until January 17, 1945 (or the eighteenth, according to other sources). On that day, the Red Army is approaching. The SS-men evacuate the camp; they organize a two-day 'death march' to the camp in Gleiwitz for the still-valid prisoners.

Later, my father will have a cold shudder on each celebration of the Auschwitz Liberation by Soviet troops: for him and his brothers this is just the point when their worst sufferings will start.

In Gleiwitz, a journey begins that he always had reported to me with mitigation, as he revealed only much later. On one day in the 1990s, he put a book of his friend Robert Francès in my hand and said: "You must read this. He has had the same experience as I did but I was not able to tell everything. Read, and you will understand."

As I knew the story, they had been in open-top freight wagons for eight or nine days, on their way to Nordhausen via Vienna, in 'pajamas,' under bitter frost and snow, without food nor drink. I knew about their endless waiting under a street bridge in Vienna, about dried-out prisoners crying for water, about pedestrians passing by who broke with their feet some icicles that fell into the wagons, causing injuries or even deaths. I knew that my father and his elder brother Camille, who travelled with him, had been among the very few survivors when the train arrived in Nordhausen. I knew that he was incapable of standing up and was carried to a repository outside the Nordhausen-Dora Concentration Camp, that his feet were frozen, for which he would suffer for all his life and could predict snow weather. He had spoken often of all this.

But what he could not reveal was that he only was able to survive with help of the corpses by which he had been protected from cold. An overwhelming horror, for him impossible to tell.

Merely the seventeen-year-old Nathan Stermann still is able to stand and walk upon arrival. He is registered in the Dora-Mittelbau Concentration Camp under the identification number 108822, as can be seen in his camp file card. Camille and Henry are left lying half-dead in former training buildings of the *Luftwaffe*, the so-called *Boelcke-Kaserne*. Nonetheless, they too are registered in Dora-Mittelbau under the numbers 108906 and 109049. The heavily disturbed railroad system and an air raid on the building prevent them from being transported to the Bergen-Belsen Camp to get there the final stroke as the SS had planned.

Saved by the shelter of a multiple bunk bed and sustained by a strawberry jam supply exploded and burnt from a bomb, Henry is discovered there by an advanced group of the US Army which had been sent ahead to urgently stop the production of V2 missiles in the Dora tunnel plant.

Camille and Henry had one last occasion to catch a glimpse of their younger brother Nathan. He had been among the camp survivors; I think the SS emptied the camp before the Americans came, and secretly murdered the remaining prisoners somewhere on their way. Anyway, Nathan has never been seen again. Not a single German archive document mentioning his destiny could be retrieved, even by applying to the international commission set up for finding persons lost in the war events.

My father had a suspicion that his beloved younger brother had been among the 1,016 victims of the mass murder when a barn near Gardelegen had been intentionally set on fire on April 13, 1945.

After the air raid, Camille thinks he is the only Stermann remained alive; he simply steps out into the German countryside. The SS capture him back and imprison him in the Camp at Wansleben. When the battlefront approaches, the prisoners are to descend into a potash mine to be murdered there. They refuse, resisting beating and menaces; subsequently, their tormentors disappear shortly before the Americans arrive.

Camille is on the walk again. He settles in a nearby farm; the scared farmers feed him for a month. Fit and restored, he arrives on June 1 by train in Paris, dressed in Bavarian-Tyrolean style.

I liked my uncle Camille. He would never stop joking and making me laugh. His favorite and most typical joke was: "Don't touch, you, with your hands full of fingers!" Reportedly, he would say *"Bonjour, Mademoiselle"* (Hello, Miss) when coming across a Catholic priest; justifying himself: "So what? The person wears a long dress and is not married."

He passed away from a heart failure during his sleep; he was only forty-four years old, leaving behind a wife and a four-year-old daughter. Who knows what nightmares haunted his sleep whereas he only told funny stories?

Let me get back to the liberation of Nordhausen-Dora. Meanwhile, a home transport for the survivors is set in place. After French prisoners of war have abandoned their priority in favor of the concentration camp survivors, Henry can travel back home by air transport on April 21, 1945. Shortly before landing in Le Bourget, he can see out of the aircraft window the nearby Drancy Camp, his place of departure. A cinema weekly-news film shows the arrival of his *Dakota*. One of the liberated prisoners is seen stumbling to the ground after stepping out on the tarmac. It is he.

Then, he is questioned by the French Army. When he is reporting about the terrible gas chambers, crematoriums and so on, he can see in a mirror an officer pointing at his own temple meaning this man is mad and speaking nonsense. At that moment, my father decides to remain silent because he has experienced the unspeakable.

Fortunately, he will not definitely keep his mouth shut on the subject. To us, his children, he will tell and explain many things. In his last years, he will also be a witness for middle and high schools, answering the pupils' questions. Additionally, he will record in 1996 a testimony (in French) for the Survivors of the Shoah Visual History Foundation. I have received and digitized a copy of this video and make duplicates for all those who knew him and are interested.

*Rémy during his testimony on July 18, 1996
(video by Survivors of the Shoah Visual History Foundation)*

From Le Bourget Air Field, Henry is brought to the *Hôtel des Saints-Pères* in *Saint-Germain-des-Prés*, a central Paris district, in which the survivors are accomodated temporarily while the *Hôtel Lutétia* is being prepared for them. During the war, the latter had been the headquarters of the German Military Intelligence.

Very upset, our father has told us the routine question of the military physician who examines him: "Well, my good man, what is wrong with you?" For my father, it had to be obvious to anybody that with these death-camp survivors weighing only half of their pre-war weights, <u>everything</u> was wrong...

And then, where to go? He had no home anymore; their apartment had been reallocated to Pétain-friendly people, the whole contents lost. Photographs, papers, furniture, utensils, all gone! As opposed to others, he did not have the lucky surprise to find his home under seal of Justice, untouched.

He drags his own thin, feeble carcass to *Rue Violet*, in the 15th Paris District, where his uncle *Alexandre* Popiolek and his aunt *Solange* reside. He does not even have the strength to open subway doors; climbing the stairs up to the first upper floor takes him nearly an hour. At his relatives' home, he is welcomed, taken care of, fed. He finds there human heartiness and will remain forever thankful (whence, as I said, my middle name).

Then he will travel by train to central France and to the Alps, to check his youngest siblings. My father liked to remind of one event. Under a raincoat, he still is wearing his striped camp clothes. During a stop at one station, some sandwiches are distributed by a charity organization. He is standing at a train door, his striped jacket visible. All sandwiches land on his compartment seat. I suspect a certain exaggeration.

How Henry Stermann gets in touch with the OSE (*Oeuvre de Secours aux Enfants*, Aid Organization for Children) is unknown to me. Perhaps when he was searching for a care solution for David and Monique. Anyway, he becomes aware that this Jewish Aid organization needs an educator for orphans of Holocaust victims.

He needs a job. After the 1945 summer vacation, I suppose, he travels to Le Mans. Méhoncourt Castle had been turned into an orphanage in which Lotte Schwarz, chief educator, is acting for the missing manager.

By instinct, my father finds a bluffing way to tame the rather rebellious teenagers. On this way, he gains Lotte's affection in such a way that they build a quasi-family relationship which includes her daughter Anna (known as *Aniouta*, later *Aniou*). I often heard him speak of them to other people as "my mother" and "my sister."

As a consequence, I would tell my classmates that I had one grandfather and three grandmothers, namely *Mutti*, *Mimi* (Magali's mother) and Lotte. As an adult, this fiction disturbed me. Now I realize that, for my father, inventing a different origin was one of the means to overcome the loss of his true parents.

Lotte Schwarz in 1982

And now, as it seems to me, I have long enough intrigued my reader with *"Rémy"* written in italics. He took this pseudonym in Le Mans because there were already two educators (I think) called *"Henri."* It was too much; to avoid confusions, he was to choose another name. He remembered that during the German Occupation somebody had provided him with a forged identity card on which his name was '*Henry Rémy*,' so he would not be detected as Jewish at police checks.

From then on, he always was called '*Rémy*,' even by his brothers and sister and other relatives who so far had known him only as 'Henry.' Merely his aunt *Solange* was an exception to this custom.

With some former children from Le Mans he will remain in friendship. So for instance the Romania-born Gilles Segal who later will become a member of the pantomime group of the famous Marcel Marceau (I have photographs of Gilles Ségal, *Jacki*, *Mutti* and me on the famous Hamburg *Landungsbrücken* (floating quays), while Marceau and his group ware playing in Hamburg). Gilles Segal further became an actor, director and play author.

In contrast to this, he had broken all links with the former orphans of the UJRE-CCE. The reason for it may be that he did not want to remember the time when he was working with you, *Maman Grète*.

When I told your story, in the first part of this book, I already described how life then continues for *Rémy*. At the time of your death, we had left him managing a servicing workshop at the Paris branch of the gas-appliance manufacturer Pain, having its headquarters in Lipsheim near Strasburg. The *Pain* brand will disappear from the marketplace in the seventies after being absorbed by their larger Alsace neighbor and competitor De Dietrich.

Early in the sixties, when we have moved from Paris to the southern suburb Fontenay-aux-Roses, he will get a promotion. A traveling salesman of the company has resigned and is to be replaced. Thanks to his good technical knowledge and proved capacities, my father is chosen. He is entrusted a large sector in western-central France, is provided with a nice company car that he also may use for our weekends and vacations. My father is so much more capable than his predecessor that he achieves similar sales figures by working only on three days each week, so that his weekend often begins on Thursdays.

New professional upheaval on July 1, 1968, immediately after the well-known Paris May Events (riots and strikes). *Aniou*, Lotte's daughter, who has become a renowned bone surgeon, has joined a group of colleagues to build and operate a private hospital. They need a manager to run the purchasing and organizational operations. *Aniou* chooses her 'brother' who first hesitates to face this demanding responsibility, but eventually accepts and is trained in other similar hospitals.

Here too he will be successful; he keeps the job until his retirement. In September 1989, when Magali also becomes pensioned, the couple retires in their southern country house in Bonnieux. This former sheep farm had been purchased by Lotte during the sixties with the intention to make her 'son' own 'a little piece of France.' For a symbolic price, she had given the estate to the couple, as a kind of inheritance. My father said once that he had lived there the most beautiful decade of his life.

During his last years, the memory transmission of the Holocaust is a central point in his preoccupations. He at last accepts the receipt of a deportee pension as a compensation of what he had suffered in the Camps. He meets other survivors, reads much about the subject, dares to tell his story, and tightens his relations with his Jewish relatives and Polish roots.

When one fine day my father was speaking to me about his many uncles and aunts, I said: "Wait a minute. I'll get a pencil and a sheet of paper." On a piece of white paper, I drew some boxes in which I put some names and dates he was telling me. And this was the foundation stone of our family tree as I have been studying it since. I was thinking my father would soon disappear and with him 'a library would burn away.' I felt an urge to be acting in his place and taking over the 'duty of remembrance.'

Was the burden of his past too heavy to bear? Was it a consequence of his excessive smoking? When I arrive in Bonnieux with my wife and son for our 2000 summer vacation, my stepmother Magali takes us aside and says to me: "Your father has cancer." Bonk! Cold shower. They just received the diagnosis after an MRI examination. Hopeless: pancreas, metastasized in his liver. Then chemotherapy, hospital, final phase, artificial coma under morphine, as long as his valiant heart holds out.

Shortly before midnight on Tuesday, November 28, 2000, he fades away, only seventy-seven years old.

During his last conscious days, I had been at his bedside and we had had a very intimate mutual understanding and cherishing, much stronger than ever before. Previously, I had always felt a certain hindering, misunderstanding, distance, his very critical judgment on me; the time when I could call him '*Papa*' was very long ago.

Perhaps I reminded him too much of that past he wanted to bury, your love, your common life, your liveliness, your smile, *Maman Grète*. He projected on me his dual vision of Germany, to him a country as admirable as repelling. He considered me 'the German of the family,' a 'sausage skin.' Besides, he used to speak pejoratively of the *Chleuhs*.[34]

All this always had left in me an uncomfortable feeling. But, in that hospital room, nothing of it remained. We were reconciled.

---

[34] Name of a tribe combated during the conquest of Morocco. In the French Slang, one of the dirty words against Germans.

Lajzer and Rojzla

The story of *Rémy*'s parents is not easy to reconstruct. Here, I have almost more open questions than answers.

The part I know a little better is about my grandmother who was born on Tuesday, February 27, 1900, as Rojzla Popiołek (known as *Roizel, Roizele*) in *Ulica Žabia* (Frog Street[35]) in Włocławek on the Vistula (German name: *Leslau*). *Popiołek* is a Polish surname and a diminutive of the word *popiół* meaning 'ash,' as a Polish workmate once explained to me. It is—by the way—borne by Jewish and Catholic families as well.

Her elder brother, Mojsze Icek, had been born little less than two years before her.[36] Their father, Wolf (*Wolek*) is

---

[35] A good omen for future emigrants to France?
[36] See Documents Section, #6.

twenty-six years old. It has been said that he has been more often at the synagogue or at rest than at his work consisting of pushing a small handcart with fish and vegetables to the Old Market, the *Stary Rynek*, and perform the sales. The efficient one is the mother of the family, Ruchla (*Ruchel, Ruchele*, in France), *née* Siarka (means 'sulfur'), twenty-five years old, originating like her husband from this town. The family will become large.

After my grandmother, only boys will be born: in 1901, Aleksander (*Sender, Alexandre* in France, to whom I owe my middle name), in 1903, Hersz (*Henri* in France), in 1904, Beer (*Bejek*), in 1906, Abram (*Avrum, Albert* in France), in 1907, Nussen Joseph (*Nathan* in France), in 1909, Jakob (*Yankel, Jacob* or *Jacques* in France), and last but not least in 1911, Nachman.

Whoops, this makes a total of nine siblings! Not lazy to fulfill his marriage duty, my great-grandfather, like all well-pious husbands. As sole daughter, Rojzla helps her mother in her household and does not attend like her brothers the rabbinical school. Therefore, she is not even able to sign her name, as noted in her marriage record of 1931.

Marriage picture of Hersz and his first cousin Jeanne, 1930:
1. Wolf, 2. Ruchla, 3. Hersz, 4. Jeanne, 5. Sender, 6. Abram, 7. Nachman,
8. Yankel/Jakob, 9. Rojzla (inserted afterwards), 10. Nussen/Nathan,
11. Mosze with son David (12), 13. Beer, (remained in Poland)

But we have not yet gone so far. As a young woman, her boyfriend is a handsome young tailor's son, Lajzer (*Leiser* in France). On November 11, 1918, the Polish Republic is established after the Soviet Revolution had freed the country from the Russian domination. As one of its first achievements, it finds nothing better than mobilizing for a war against the Bolsheviks at the side of the 'White' Russians.

In my father's view, under the Czar, the members of the Jewish Community were much too despised to receive the honor of a military enrollment. In contrast to this, the young Poland recruits all its young male citizens, Jews included. However, many young men do not want to comply and flee their flag. Lajzer is one of them. Mojsze Icek, Rojzla's elder

193

brother, probably too. We will see later why I express it this way.

At this point of the story, I cannot tell if Lajzer and Rojzla are fiancés, religiously married, or administratively nothing to each other. Whatever their status may be, both of them take the flight and leave their country to the west. Their destination is Paris. Why? Like many other emigrants, they have planned to use previously emigrated relatives as a landing base.

And indeed, Ruchla, *née* Siarka has a brother, a tailor, who more than twenty years before had settled in Paris as Alexandre Sciarke. Together with his wife Adèle, who is also from Wlocławek, they have three daughters and a son, plus—I think—a girl with a heart failure who died early; all born in Paris. Another girl will be born in 1920. This couple is more or less a bridgehead and central point for all Jewish immigrants from Wlocławek in Paris and they are active managers of the 'Friends of Wlocławek' Society.

According to what has been said among relatives, my grandparents, in lack of money, might have made a travel break in Germany, perhaps in or near Berlin, perhaps at a general's home where they might have been working as a gardener and a cook. I report all this with triple conditional and tweezers.

Without immigration papers and Lajzer thinking he was wanted by the Polish authorities for desertion, it has been said that they crossed the French border illegally and secretly, perhaps even robbed by their smugglers.

Certain is it that on some fine day around 1920 they arrive at her uncle's small apartment in Paris 3, in *Cité Dupetit-Thouars*. It has been said that there was a large armchair in which all Polish immigrants would spend their first night. I have not the faintest idea by which means my grandparents managed to reside in *Impasse Putigneux*, Paris 4, as stated on Camille's birth certificate. By a strange coincidence, this small *cul-de-sac* has been removed since, and replaced by the Paris Shoah Memorial.

What I can say, however, is that they need resident's and worker's papers to live normally. It has come to their knowledge that there exists a kind of White-Russian Consulate in exile, where the October-Revolution refugees can apply when they have lost their documents. My grandparents make use of this possibility.

Nonetheless, there was an obstacle: Lajzer still felt wanted by the Poles and therefore refrained from indicating his true personal data. The reader may have noticed that so far I have written no surname for my paternal grandfather. In my father's opinion, his father would have taken a typical French family name, in order to better melt into the French population, but he knew none.[37] This is why he might have chosen a surname as different from his Polish one as he could. The officer might have noted what he had understood from Lajzer's Yiddish-Polish gobbledygook, resulting in 'Stermann'.

This version seems little credible to me; why should a Russian—or a Frenchman working for Russians—use a German spelling with a double 'n' at the end? I can rather

---

[37] See also the joke at the end of Chapter "444 Poplar Street."

imagine Lajzer grabbed this name and spelling while residing in Germany, perhaps from his benefactor.

Rojzla, by contrast, applied with her true 'Popiolek' surname but her given name (which means 'little rose') was changed into *Rachel* (in fact, the same name as her mother, Ruchla). And both of them had to be accounted for as Russian refugees, therefore they changed their birth places into Kharkov (nowadays Kharkiv, Ukraine), in many French documents erroneously spelled *Karkoff*.

He declares the given name *Leiser*, which in some French documents will appear as *Lazare*. Up to now, I have used a Polish spelling for him, without any certainty that this might be right.

My father had the suspicion that they had stated higher ages than their true ones. As a matter of fact, he was right in his mother's case because in France she was supposedly born on May 10, 1898, this is almost two years earlier as indicated in the Polish Inhabitant Register, as my research has yielded.

Based on the birth date of October 1, 1896, shown on my grandfather's documents, if the same shifting applies, he might perhaps have been born around 1898. Not guaranteed at all, of course.

And why do I not know it better? Because my grandfather was in such a fear of the Polish authorities that he never dared to reveal his true identity, not even to his own children. He was reported, anyway, as someone who did not speak much. Was he perhaps therefore a *'Leiser'*?[38]

For all reasons above, the reader will understand why my genealogical research is not getting forward regarding his ancestors. No surname (almost: see his sister's story in "444 Poplar Street" Chapter below), uncertain given name, no birth date, birth place also uncertain, parents' names perhaps pure imagination, Polish archives partly destroyed. The traces have mightily blurred away.

In the years after their immigration, the remaining family of my grandmother now called *Rachel* also will settle in Paris, except Beer. The latter, a waiter in the most fashionable café of Włocławek, married, will exchange a last series of letters with his brother Hersz in the pre-war year 1939, in which he mentions that he lacks the necessary means to travel to Paris and that he wants to move to Warsaw. In the chaos of the war he and his wife totally disappeared. I found no trace of them, neither among Holocaust Victims nor in the ghetto of Warsaw among Resistance fighters, victims, escaped survivors.

Regarding the oldest Popiolek sibling, the furrier Mojsze Icek, his French papers designate him as *Maurice Popilok*, a Russian refugee, born on May 1895 in Odessa. That makes me think that he too illegally left Poland deserting the army. He seems to have obtained his papers by the same means as his brother-in-law and sister (my paternal grandparents—are you still following?), increasing his official age by three years. Or was he perhaps even the first one to do so, and did he show them the way?

---

[38] *'Leiser'* can be understood as 'silent' in German and Yiddish.

He will anyway, like his brother *Alexandre*, manage to hide during the war, avoiding arrest, abduction, and possibly murder.

And while I am on the subject, here is the fate of the other brothers. In August 1942, in Dijon, the capital of Burgundy, the tailor Hersz—as his son Claude told me—let himself be arrested on purpose at the Inner-French Demarcation Line checkpoint, to protect his youngest brother Nachman from being caught. He will perish in Auschwitz: Transport number 45 on November 11, 1942, from Drancy Camp.

Nachman, on his side, who had become a street vendor in Lyons, was not safe forever, unfortunately. Eventually also arrested, he is among the missing men of the disciplinary Transport number 73 which exceptionally did not go to Auschwitz but to several camps, forts and prisons in Lithuania and Estonia, after having departed from Drancy on May 15, 1944. He leaves behind a widow, Marguerite (*Tante Margot*), divorced, who comes from a Catholic family in Normandy and runs a fur shop in Paris.

The brothers *Nathan*, tailor, whose London-born wife Cecilia was abducted from Drancy to Auschwitz with Transport number 9 on July 22, 1942, with no return, and *Jacques*, a hairdresser married to a pianist, are both arrested—after having been summoned in a written form in the framework of the notorious 'green-bill roundup'—and interned in the Camp at Beaune-la-Rolande near Orléans on May 14, 1941.

On each file card is stamped the reason for their internment: "Surplus in the national economy." They work in an external commando at the farmer Barnault's estate in the nearby Auxy. Around August 6, 1941, their 'employer' says to them: "Do you see the freight trains being formed over there? There is a rumor that you are to be sent to Germany for working. Tomorrow, I shall turn my back for a while. If I do not see you anymore afterwards, I shall not give immediate alarm."

Both brothers are perplexed. *Nathan* chooses to flee. His file card bears the note: "Escaped on August 7, 1941." *Jacques,* who had learnt his hairdresser occupation in Germany, thinks it makes little difference whether he is to work in France or Germany. He dares not take the chance to be caught and punished. If only he had known where Transport number 5 of June 28, 1942 would take him...

His brother, on his part, knows that his childhood friend from Wlocławek, Marcel Dabrowski, is accommodated not too far in Issoudun, secretly crosses the Demarcation Line in Saint-Florent-sur-Cher and is hidden with his friend and family.

Raymonde Jabouille, a young Communist resistant, provides food to hidden Jews deprived of food tickets. She falls in love with my granduncle; they will live together and get three children. *Nathan* succumbs to a heart attack on April 30, 1959. He never wanted (nor could as long as his missing wife was not declared dead) marry Raymonde; he was in fear that the whole thing might happen again and his new family experience a new catastrophe.

Let us now get back to my grandparents. Shortly before the birth of their fourth child, David—yet another boy!—, they clarify their administrative situation by marrying on Tuesday, March 17, at the Townhall of the 15th Paris District.

I am not informed whether they did so by their own initiative or somebody advised them, so that their son this time really was born as legitimate. So it happened that their three first-born were provided with such contradicting notes on their birth certificates.[39]

Just as it happened for me, my father has known his mothers' parents but not the ones of his father who, to my knowledge, never travelled to France. *Leiser* had a sister, Esther, who emigrated before the First World War to the United States. I shall speak of her more in detail in "444 Poplar Street," Chapter, further down.

At a date unknown to me, and considering the Hitler danger in Europe, she has sent to the Paris Stermann family affidavits and money so they would be able to join her in the USA.

My grandfather feared the Poles, whom he often had seen brutal against Jews. But in contrast he admired the Germans, having found them much further developed and polite. Therefore he was not afraid of them. *Rachel* and he felt good in France; they did not want to change countries and restart everything from the beginning again. They should have. However, they preferred to use the money for new furniture which, unfortunately, they will not enjoy too long.

Then comes war, Occupation, fascist Vichy Regime, mandatory filing at the police office; in reverence of the authorities, they comply. Mandatory wearing of the infa-

---

[39] See beginning of previous chapter.

mous Jew star; they comply. Work and trade prohibition hit Jews: impossible to continue working as a contractor for garment makers. Their elder sons sustain the whole family with illegal work.

On Thursday, July 16, 1942, at dawn, loud knocking at the apartment door of 15 *Rue Bargue*. The parents are no French citizens, they must follow the French policemen to the nearby *Vel d'Hiv* indoor velodrome. Their five children remain at home by themselves. On the day after, their second son Henry tries to find out what has become of his parents. He sneaks up to the cycling race hall, tries to get information. But the security forces chase away all curious people.

Another youngster asks him what time it is, because as a pious observant Jew he does not feel allowed to ride on the subway after sunset on that Friday, start of *Shabbat*. My father would often give this example to criticize the exaggerated strictness of religious commandments. How could they in such a situation be more important than the fate of this young man's family?

The fate of my paternal grandparents consists of Pithiviers Camp (near Orléans), Transports number 13 of July 31 (for him) number 16 of August 6, 1942 (for her), respectively; terminal station: Auschwitz and its smoking chimneys.

Rich marriage in Merlebach
or
Should one believe in family legends?

Here comes a narrative as tragic as enlightening about my granduncle Abram Popiolek. This was an occasion of comparing a legend told among my relatives with fragments of truth yielded by my research.

First the story, as my father used to tell it. His uncle Abram had had, in Merlebach, Lorraine, "a rich marriage," and established there. While fleeing before the German invasion in 1940, he witnessed his wife and child ("I think it was a girl") being killed, causing his lifetime insanity.

After the war, Henry, who had not yet become *Rémy*, paid his uncle a visit at Paris *Sainte-Anne* psychiatric Hospital. He would recognize nobody, nor utter a single word. When provided with a needle, he would mime a tailor at work. Since no communication was possible anymore, the visits of relatives to the poor fool became less and less frequent. Much later, on one of his visits, my father was told that his uncle was not there anymore and nobody could tell where he had been transferred to. So, he did not know what had become of Abram.

My research was lengthy and comprehensive. I had to deal with the Berton burying company near the South-Paris Bagneux Cemetery, with the Civil Registration office of Freyming-Merlebach, with the French National Library to access the file about persecution of Jews, with *Sainte-Anne* Hospital by the means of my uncle David's son-in-law

Jacques who was a psychiatric doctor there. By telephone and paper mail I have corresponded with Abram's family-in-law in Lorraine.

I could not discover everything, but here are the elements I could find out. Avram's father-in-law was a gentlemen's tailor in Merlebach, a coal mining area. They would ride their bicycles along the streets with miner housings and offer tailor-made Sunday suits. This occupation provided a modest prosperity, far from a great wealth. Exit the "rich marriage."

At the beginning of 1940, several months before the May-June invasion by *Wehrmacht* and *Luftwaffe*, the authorities of border territories decide an administrative evacuation of civilians to inner France. Some relatives by marriage from Metz, for instance, are displaced to Angoulême in Charente Department, others to Châtellerault in Vienne Department. The inhabitants of Merlebach are evacuated to Civray, a small town also in Vienne, a little further to the south.

Soura Riwka

Although it is true that Abram (*Albert*) and his wife Soura Riwka (*Sonia*) have a child, it is a pretty little boy named Victor, born on Sunday, January 8, 1939 in Merlebach. In Civray, they live for around three years in a small house with two upper stories, located 5 *Rue du Moulin Neuf* ('New Mill Street'), a part of a little row. Neighbors from Merlebach live next door.

The Jews arrested in the French Occupied Zone were too few in the eyes of the Nazis. Therefore, the Vichy authorities organized in the 'non-occupied' Zone additional round-ups. One of them occurred in Civray in mid-October 1942.

Non-Jewish neighbors propose to take care of Little Victor, three years old, light curls. He cries, tramples, does not want to leave his mother. As a consequence, he will be taken with her and other Jewish refugees, imprisoned in Poitiers together with people arrested in other locations, then transferred to Drancy. From there, Transport number 42 on November 6, 1942, into death.

Victor

I had some difficulties to find them on the microfilm of the camp card file because their names were spelled *Popolick*.

Popiolek, as he was called in Merlebach, already had been known as insane while his wife and son were still alive. One of his relatives by marriage told me once on the telephone: "Popiolek? He was *Meshugge*."[40] Reportedly, on his wife's request he had been for a while in care of the hospital in Poitiers after furious madness crises, which might have preserved him from being arrested. Herewith vanishes the myth of his insanity being caused by the Nazi barbarity.

Raymonde Jabouille, the companion of his brother *Nathan*, thinks that, back from fetching something, Abram had witnessed his wife and son being arrested without showing himself, and that he had then tried to join his brothers in Paris.

I have taken what comes now from his hospital file,

---

[40] Yiddish term meaning 'fool,' sometimes also used in German.

which I possess. Around October 17, 1942, Abram is near Austerlitz train station, where—among others—trains from Poitiers arrive in Paris. He must have caused some public nuisance because on a written order of the local Police commissionaire he is interned in the nearby *Salpétrière* Hospital. A psychiatric referral is undersigned on October 19 by Professor Lévy-Valensi; the patient is transferred on the following day into his department at *Sainte-Anne* Hospital.

The patient file discards every doubt about the cause of his insanity: "Progressive general paresis." On my own, I would not have decoded this diagnosis, but my psychiatric cousin by marriage has explained it to me. This was the shameful expression behind which was hidden ... the third stage of syphilis. At his arrival, he is described as "violent, agitated."

On a transfer order bill dated May 11, 1952, he is stated to be calm, obedient, silent and eligible for a placement in a family. He is transferred to a hospital in Ainay-le-Château in Allier Department. Certificate dated June 9 and 29, 1952: "General paresis treated. Mutism, but seems to understand questions, answers them with head movements, understands and executes orders. Is calm and obedient."

By Prefect command of Cher Department dated December 27, 1952, an administrative accommodation in Chezal-Benoît, a nursing home owned by the Seine Department (to which Paris belonged)[41] is prescribed: "Progressive paresis. Mental weakness. Absolute mutism." He will meet his death

---

[41] After a 1964 territorial reform, Paris became a Department by itself.

there on January 12, 1970, from a "terminal evolution" and "influenza state" with high fever lasting since October.

Among the Popiolek siblings, Abram will have died last, without any relative being aware. When I reported on the telephone to Raymonde Jabouille that her companion's brother had been living only ten miles away from Issoudun without them knowing it, it gave her a shock.

The moral of this story is that one should be particularly prudent with family legends. Often, some elements are fancy additions. What is not known is imagined, a novel is created that later will be considered the truth. A persistent 'truth,' because even after they have heard the real elements, some family members keep telling the forged story they like better.

This said, several unsolved mysteries remain. How did Abram eventually escape being arrested in Civray? How could he, a Jew, cross the Demarcation Line unhindered? How could he, during the German Occupation of France, remain in *Sainte-Anne* Hospital, being a Jew and incurably mentally ill, while indeed the Nazis unashamedly emptied hospitals, knowing moreover that even Professor Lévy-Valensi himself perished in Auschwitz?

444 Poplar Street

Let us now leave the relatives of my paternal grandmother and concentrate on my grandfather. I shall evoke one of the greatest joys provided by my family research, which however is also connected with a great regret.

I shall start again with what my father told me when I was filling with boxes the already evoked sheet of paper that became the seed of my whole quest. He told me that he had an aunt in the USA, in Philadelphia, a sister of his father's with whom there had been a letter exchange.

And because on that day I begin to be interested in our family history, I start to regret that I did not listen to my father in July–August 1968, when in my school vacation I had a summer job as a deck help on a Hamburg-America-Line cargo ship for one round-trip to the East Coast of North America. He had told me that, if I called at the port of Philadelphia, I should try to contact his aunt. Although we did make a stop in that harbor, I had been too shy with my sixteen years of age and too little motivated for this enquiry.

Well, well, that is past. As I often say, one's future can be changed but one's past cannot. Moreover, I have known more recently that this aunt passed away as early as in 1965, three year before my trip.

So, my father tells me the story already shortly evoked above about his aunt from Philadelphia, the travelling money, affidavits and so on. And he said to me that for all these years he had been able to keep in his memory his aunt's address, which he had seen on the letter envelopes: *Goldman, 444 Poplar Street* in Philadelphia. As an epilogue to the story, he told me that neighbors at *Rue Bargue* had reported that after Paris Liberation in 1944 a US soldier had come there and asked for the Stermann family. He had received the answer that they all had been abducted and had disappeared.[42]

At the end of his life, *Rémy* had become keener and keener to discover the secret of his original surname. In his opinion, his Philadelphia aunt had no need to hide her maiden name and therefore the Goldman family could deliver the key to this mystery.

This is why I picked up the trail. It was not an easy task: a very common surname, no given names (my father had forgotten that the first name of his aunt was Esther), merely an address at an uncertain time between both wars. My first attempt consisted of issuing some requests on the internet with a search engine, using some thoroughly chosen keywords. Far too many Goldman individuals have I found, however not a single one at the right address. And then I had the idea of putting the search the other way round.

What if our relatives on the other side of the Atlantic were searching for us? I have set up my homepage on the World-Wide Web (michel.stermann.free.fr), with a text in three languages telling the story in question, with some photographs and the title: "Who can tell? Searching for my American relatives." I have imbedded several keywords in

---

[42] At that time, all Stermann children were either hidden in the countryside or deported.

the metadata to increase the chances that my relatives find my page with a search engine.

Simultaneously, I have searched on specialized Internet sites, such as those for Genealogy; I have posted an advertisement on an Israel-based Web service specialized in finding missing people after the Holocaust, filled out a search form of the International Red-Cross, and so forth.

These efforts brought many contacts, often pleasant and interesting, but for years nothing concrete. My homepage had at least the unexpected utility that, instead of telling everyone the same story from the beginning, I just needed to send a hypertext link to it.

In a nutshell, here are the circumstances that eventually lead me to success. A German lady, a volunteer search help for missing persons, noticed my advertisement and took an interest in my case. After a copious exchange, she drew my attention to a very lively Web forum focused on family research in Philadelphia. I posted my request there. A first volunteer sent me a scanned pre-war telephone directory page with the entry "M. Goldman" and the right address.

First victory: I knew that my father had not been mistaken and his uncle's given name started with an 'M.' Afterwards, I received a sheet from the recently publicly released 1930 census with Meyer Goldman, his wife Esther, their children Louis, Franck and Dora, 444 Poplar Street. Now, I knew the composition of the whole family.

Without any success, I wrote a letter to all Frank-Goldman addresses I could find in a Philadelphia on-line telephone directory, with the thought that Louis was too old to remain alive and Dora would have a new surname by marriage. Another waiting period.

Then, a lady on the forum, a professional genealogist, awoke and realized I was from Paris, remembering that she had spent a part of her childhood there. I suddenly had become interesting for her; we exchanged about Paris and the French language. After quite a while she started searching for me and discovered the marriage certificates for all three Goldman children, including Dora's married name: Chant. And because there are fewer Chants than Goldmans in Philadelphia, I found Dora's youngest son in the telephone directory and placed a call right away. His wife picked up, not realizing; only the Poplar Street address rang a bell in her, as well as the name Frank Goldman, and this is how the contact with my American relatives was established in May 2003.

Rémy's *aunt and uncle from Philadelphia*

One year later, I crossed the Atlantic with my son and we met our relatives face to face. Dora unfortunately had passed away but Frank and even the older Louis (or Lewis) were still alive, almost ninety years old. We met with them and their descendents.

Not one of them ever had been searching for us, by the way. The next generation was not even aware that there was a French branch in the family tree. We also were not able to establish who might have been the GI who reportedly had enquired in *Rue Bargue*, not even whether or not such an event had taken place at all.

There remains the mystery of our real name. My father already had had a clue in 1965 at Bagneux Cemetery near Paris when his brother Camille was buried. There had been old members of the "Friends of Włocławek" Society that owned the grave. *Rémy* had asked them. Yes, two among them had known in the old days the boy friend of Rojzla. What the hell was his name? Shulamovitch; no, Shulimovitch; no, Shlamovitch... and so on. He came from a respectable family, said they.

I knew also that the only occasion on which my father saw his father weep was after receiving a letter informing Leiser of his father's death. I have no idea of the date, before the Second World War, of course. It had also been known in the Popiolek family that this grandfather had been very pious. If true, why was it not Leiser's case?

I had travelled to Philadelphia carrying all these questions with me. When I asked Lewis and Frank Goldman about their mother's maiden name, they could not remember it. When I suggested "Shulamovitch," Frank said: "Yes, something like that." At the home of my American relatives there was a family photograph; I recognized Leiser as a teenager, Esther as a young woman, obviously with their parents and also a little girl, probably a younger sister of whom I had never heard.

*The photo found in Philadelphia:
Rémy's Father and aunt with parents and unknown sister*

Only comment by Frank and Lewis: "That picture comes from Europe." The name 'Wlocławek' did not ring a bell; in Poland, they only knew Warsaw.

There remains one document, which I have not mentioned so far: the passenger list of the steamship 'Armenia' of the Hamburg-America-Line, arriving at Philadelphia on December 27, 1913. It bears the names of Nachman Schlakar (the original name of Meyer Goldman, born in Bessarabia, now Moldavia) and of his wife Esther, unfortunately without her maiden name indicated. Origin: Warsaw. "Name and address of nearest relative or friend in country whence alien came": Itzig Schulimowitz, friend, Warsaw.

Surprising, that name. Could the husband's 'friend' not have been one of the wife's relatives? But nothing is sure at this stage. A couple of years later, I receive an e-mail message from Ellen, the oldest daughter of Lewis Goldman. She had come across old notes of hers from the time when, with the help of her father (who still had a clear mind, then), she had started to draw a family tree. As maiden name for her grandmother Esther, she had written "*Schulamovitch.*" This time, I am sure. Two completely different sources have yielded the same information: the old men at my uncle Camille's burial and my American relatives.

And if the reader was careful at the beginning of this chapter, he or she will ask me: "How about your great regret?" Well, it is that my father passed away in 2000, before I could report him my achievement. I comfort myself with the thought that, nevertheless, he had received a clue to our true name, even though he was not sure of it. Anyway, I would not have been able to find the Goldman family before the 1930 Census had been made available to the public.

There remains that I still cannot research about my paternal grandfather's ancestors. His given name is uncertain, the spelling of our surname approximate, I have no birth date, no certainty whether he was born in Włocławek, Warsaw or anywhere else. These indications are not sufficient.

To close this chapter with a drop of humor, I cannot resist the temptation of telling a joke *Rémy* liked particularly, about which my US relatives laughed loud, knowing that Nachman Schlakar had his name changed for 'Meyer Goldman' in the United States. The scene takes place on Ellis

Island. Jewish immigrants from Eastern Europe are standing in a waiting line at the Immigration counter. One of them asks his neighbor:

"I have a particularly conspicuous Jewish surname. In this country, I would like to bear a typical American name, so I can start a new life without being ridiculous. Unfortunately, I know none; could you please suggest me one?"

"Why don't you just say 'Rockefeller'?" says the other.

"What a strange name! So hard to remember!"

After a long wait, it is our man's turn. When the Immigration officer asks for his name, he beats his own forehead and cries out in Yiddish: *"Oi, shoin fargesen!"* (Oh, already forgotten!). Unfazed, the officer writes down...:

"John Ferguson."

Conclusion

Well, *Maman Grète*, this is what I wanted to tell you about yourself, about your direct and by-marriage relatives. Naturally, it often is just a summary, but the essentials from the 'extraordinary stories' known to me are there.

For those who would like to know all ancestors I have discovered, I have deposited the contents of my database on a genealogical World-Wide-Web site at address *www.geneanet.org* and keep it up-to-date. In my developments above, I have endeavored to be open and honest, to avoid telling blurry or exaggerated things, without concealing my knowledge gaps and presumptions.

I am conscious that these narratives contain many dramas and sufferings. I hope my readers are not excessively shaken and have found an interest in their reading, including historians among them.

Because, in my opinion, Genealogy and family research belong to historic science, as its private branch, so to speak. The tools are similar: Testimonies, written documents, research studies, analyses, and so on. Both knowledge domains are intermingled and mutually nurturing.

And it appears to me that the qualities indispensable for historians and family researchers are the same: honesty, accuracy, endurance, caution when dealing with legends and ready-made ideas, ability to decipher, to decode, to understand.

Even though no 'objectivity' is possible. Since like a historian's my work is necessarily dyed with my feelings, my culture, my interests.

In harmony with the ideals of my predecessors within my family, I express the wish that mankind could become more reasonable, so that the horrors evoked here are not repeated. The present does not seem to fulfill my dreams, but should one therefore give up the perspective of a better, more human world?

DOCUMENTS

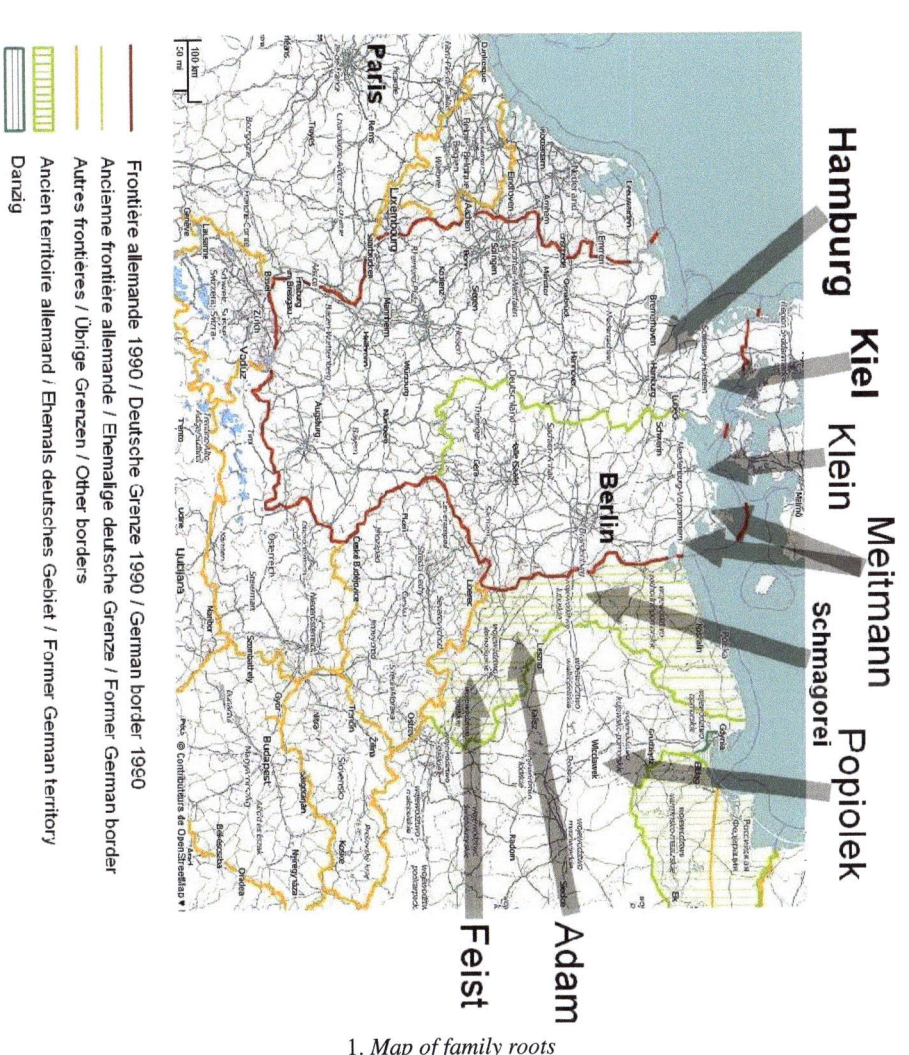

1. *Map of family roots*

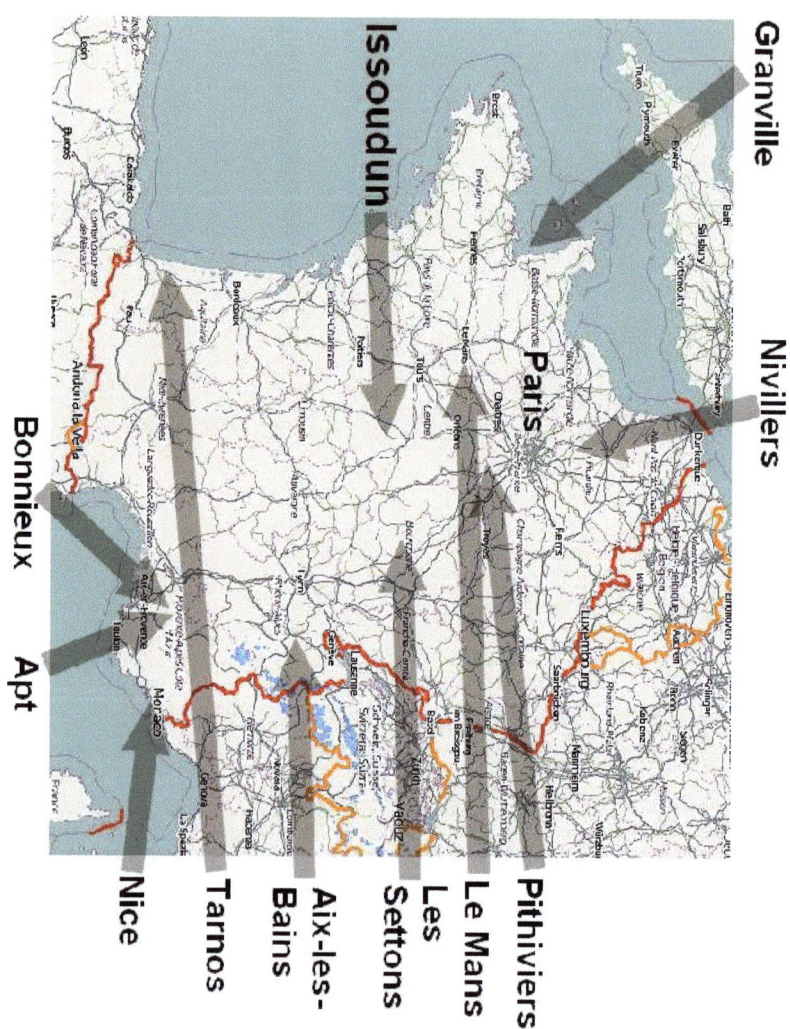

2. Map of the main locations in France mentioned

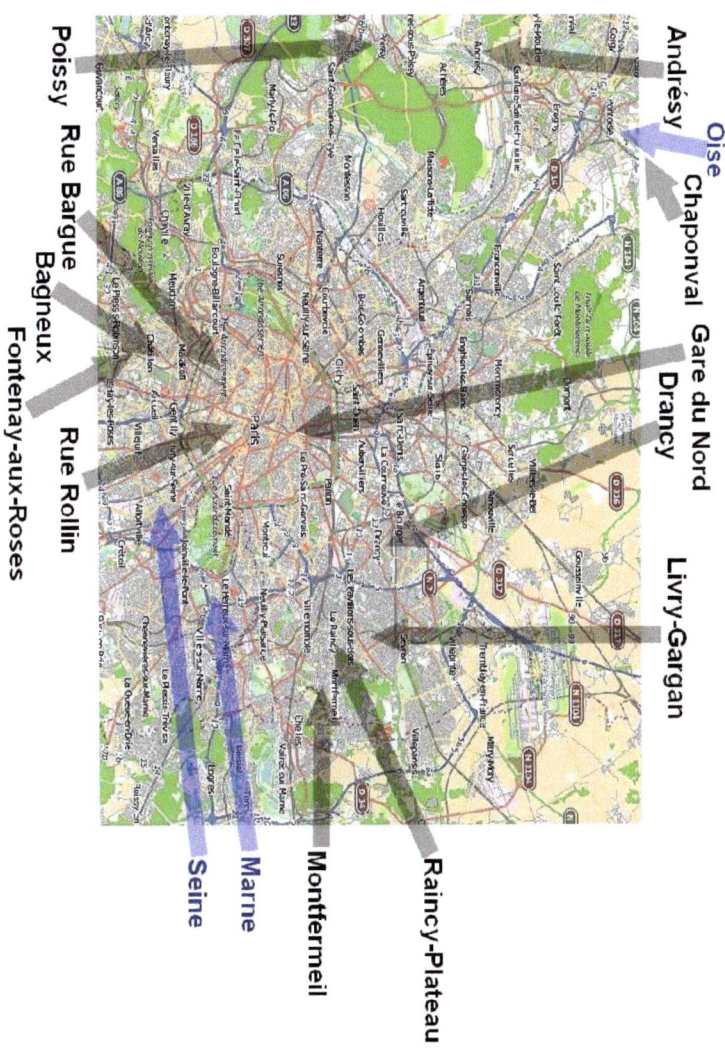

3. Map of the main locations in and around Paris mentioned

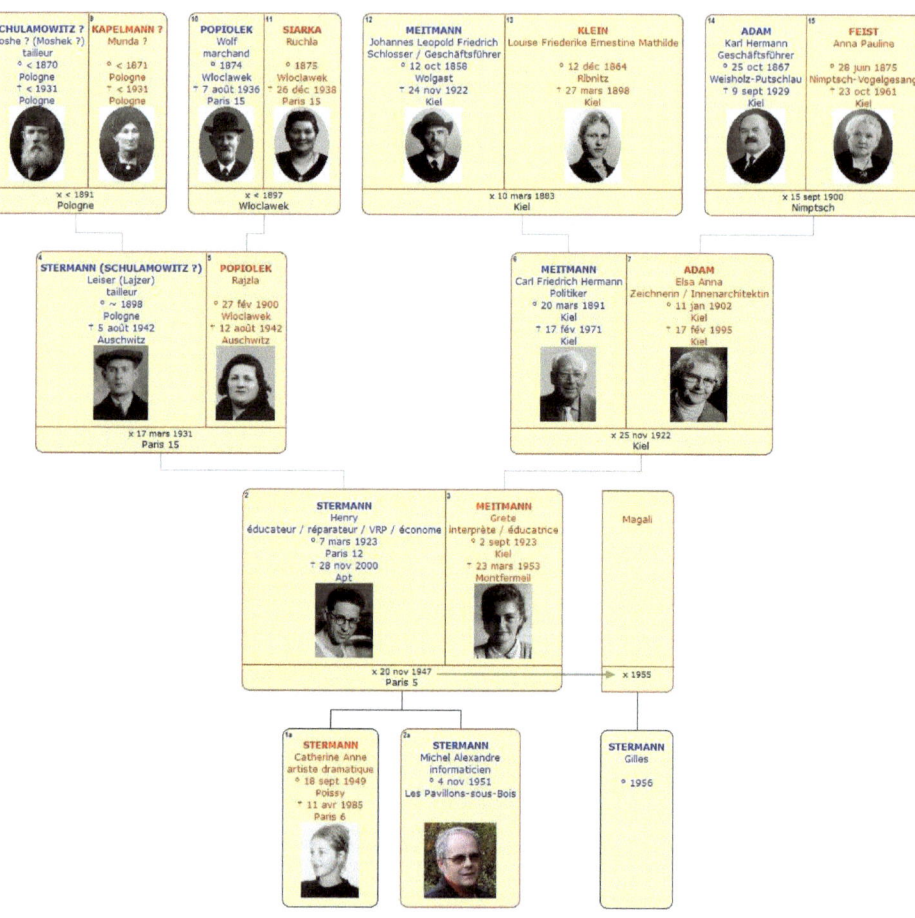

4. 4-generation family tree

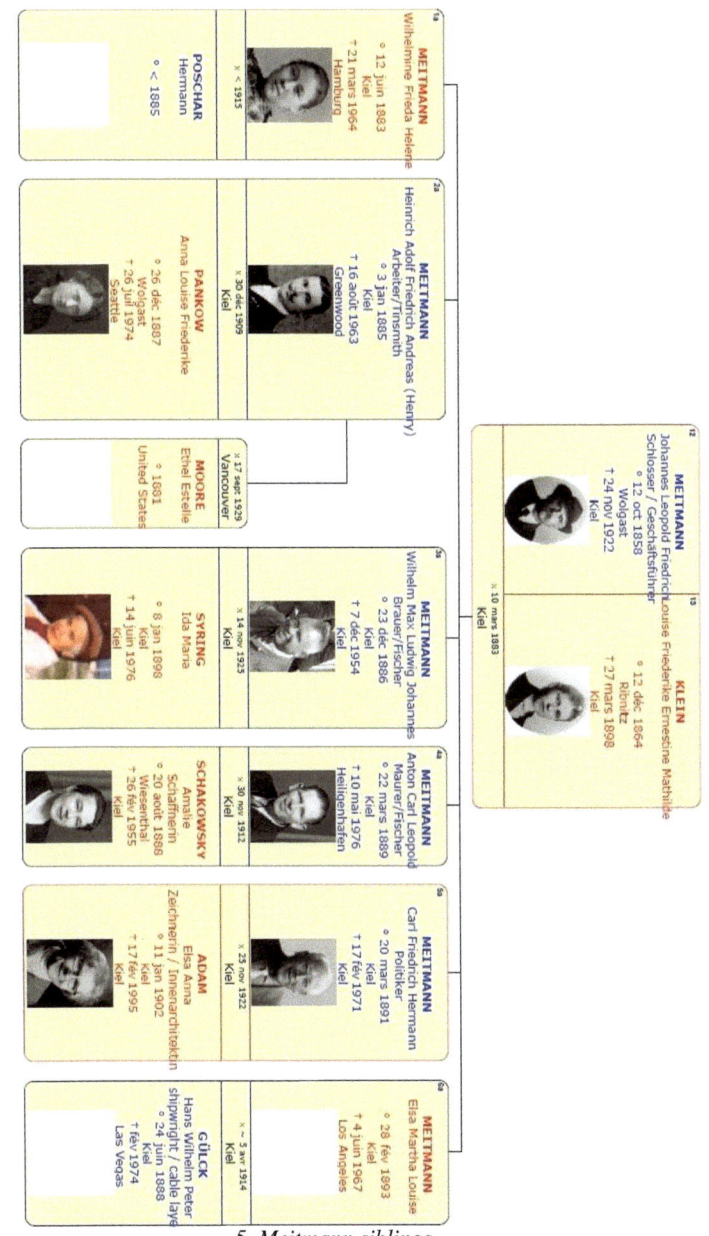

5. Meitmann siblings

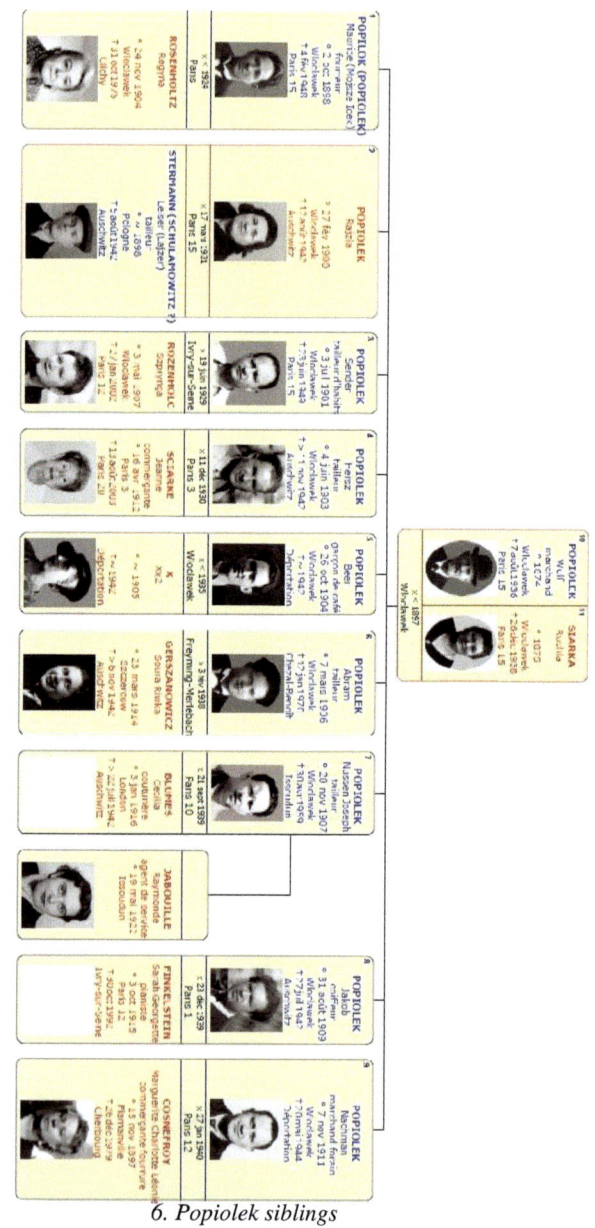

6. Popiolek siblings

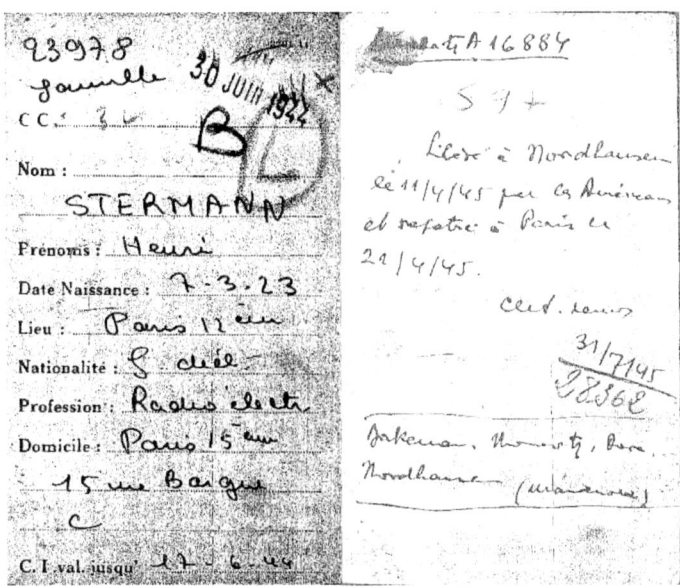
7. Drancy Camp file card, Henry Stermann

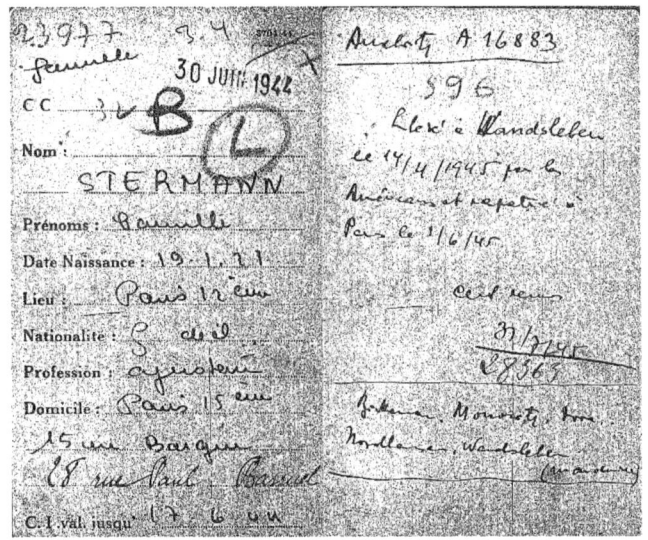
8. Drancy Camp file card, Camille Stermann

9. Drancy Camp file card, Nathan Stermann

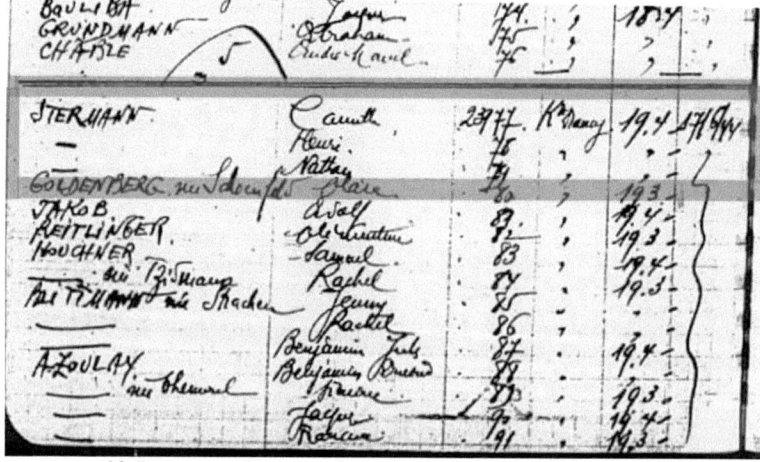

10 Fragment of Drancy Camp register dated June 17, 1944

11. Drancy Camp, receipt for cash deposit dated June 17, 1944

NOM : S T E R M A N N
PRÉNOMS : Leiser
Date et lieu de naissance : 1/10/96 à KHARKOFF
N° du Dossier juif : 37182
SEXE : masc
NATIONALITÉ : rér russe
PROFESSION : tailleur sal
ADRESSE : 15 r Bargue PARIS 15°

SITUATION de famille : marié
CONJOINT : juive

	Prénoms	Date et lieu de naissance	Nationalité
ENFANTS de moins de 15 ans et à charge	NATHAN	1927	Frse
	DAVID	1931	Frse
	MONIQUE	1936	Frse

INFIRMITÉS :

SERVICES de GUERRE :

SITUATION administrative de l'étranger : arrêté le 16.7.42

N° du casier central : 97115
REMARQUES PARTICULIÈRES :

265-E — Imp. Chaix (B). — 1591-41

12. Police file card, Leiser Stermann

13. File card, Leiser Stermann

14. Pithiviers Camp file card, Leiser Stermann

15. Pithiviers Camp file card, Rachel Stermann

16. Drancy Camp file card, Hersz Popiolek

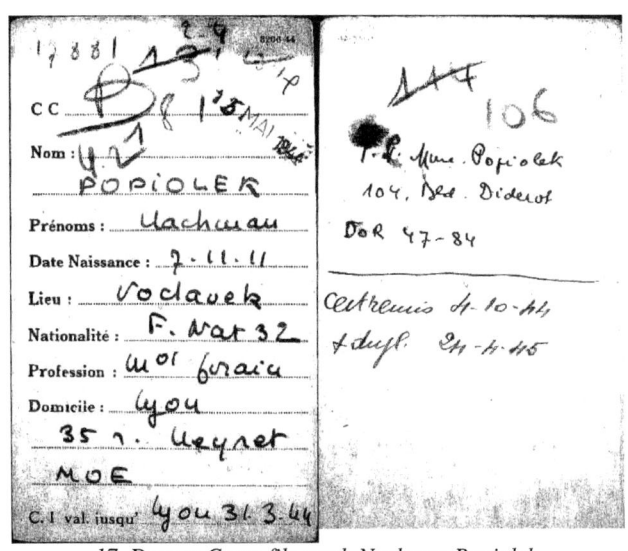

17. Drancy Camp file card, Nachman Popiolek

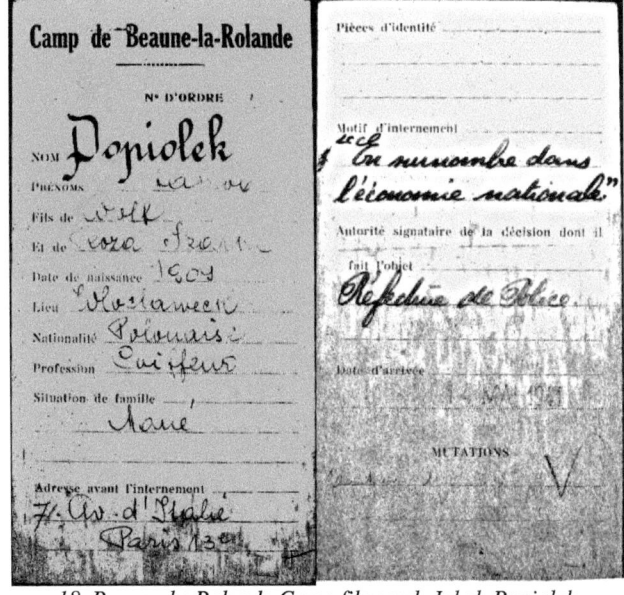

18. Beaune-la-Rolande Camp file card, Jakob Popiolek

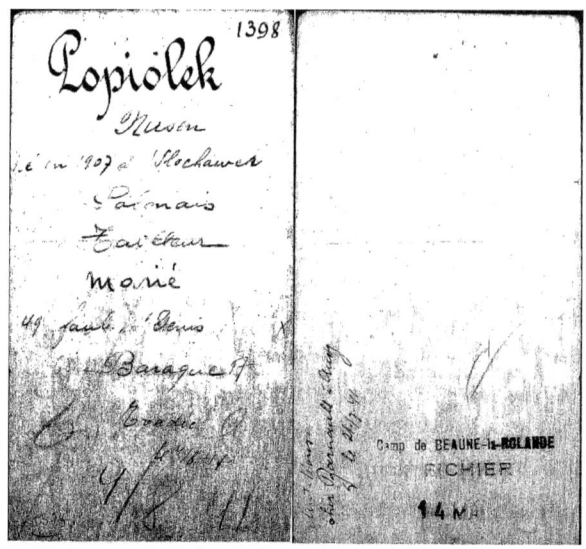

19. Beaune-la-Rolande Camp file card, Nusen Popiolek

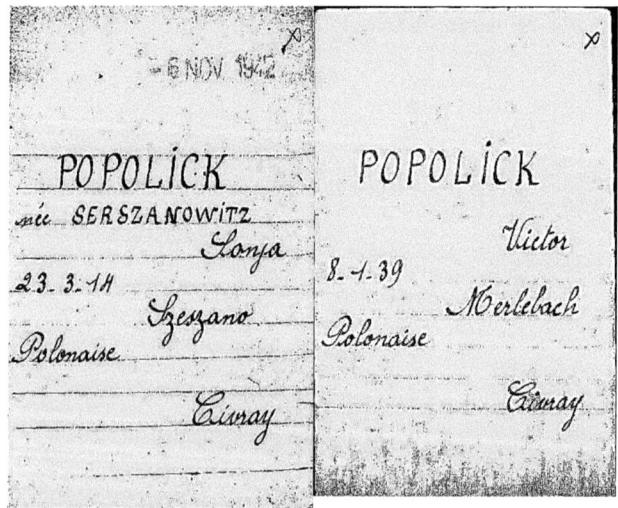

20-21. File cards for the wife and child of Abram Popiolek

22. Orphanage terrace in Nice,
first page from Grete's letter dated March 30, 1948, fountain pen, dark-blue ink

23. Grete's and Rémy's room in Nice, drawing by Grete, in her letter dated April 7, 1948, color pencils

*24. "Entering Lychen", watercolor by Grete, July 1940,
Source: Historic Psychiatry Archive of Charité Hospital, Berlin*

*25." Lychen, view on Wurl Lake", watercolor by Grete, July 1940,
Source: Historic Psychiatry Archive of Charité Hospital, Berlin*

26. Watercolor by Grete, July 1940,
Source: Historic Psychiatry Archive of Charité Hospital, Berlin

Thanks

This book would not have come about—at least under this form—without the collaboration and support of many persons. My very special thanks to:

- Katy Hazan who put me in contact with the former CCE orphans,
- All former children and educators who shared with me their memories of my parents, among which
  - Zette Lunet, Benjamine Gerbal, Rosette Siclis, Esther and Micha Brym, Roda Kornblum, Bernadette Pszenica, Hélène Waysenson ...
  - Marcel Jablonka who drove me to translate Grete's letters into French and to write this book,
  - Daniel Baron who convinced me that I was able to do it,
- Ève Line Blum-Cherchevsky who drove me to lead further my research on my granduncle Nachman Popiolek,
- Raymonde Jabouille for her comprehensive information and photographic documentation about my granduncle Nussen Popiolek,
- Jeannette Gersanois for her information and photographs about the family and family-in-law of my granduncle Abram Popiolek,
- My cousins Évelyne and Jacques, who provided me with his patient file,

- My first cousin once removed Claude Popiolek who showed me the way with his own book,
- My uncle David who offered me the precious 'blue book' published by former CCE orphans,
- Dr. Rainer Herrn of the Historic Psychiatry Archive of Charité Hospital, Berlin who enabled my access to Grete's patient file,
- Elvira Funk-Schaier who drove me to write a German version,
- Gabi and Helge Neumann who did its proofreading,
- My British second cousin Carmen who read my German draft with a critical eye and gave me advices,
- Ainslie Campbell who did a thorough professional copyediting of the present English version,
- Joyce Gardner who put me in contact with her and promoted my book,
- My mother-in-law Odette who lent me an careful ear when I read to her the French draft I was writing in her home in Summer 2015,
- My maternal grandparents who did not dispose of anything, so that I could inherit their family archive,
- My wife Danielle who supported me and did a careful proofreading of the French draft ...

... as well as all those whom I have forgotten to mention and whose pardon I am humbly begging.

Bibliography

Books in French:
- Baron, Daniel, *La vie Douce-Amère d'un Enfant Juif*, éd. l'Harmattan 2010
- Francès, Robert, *Un Déporté Brise son Silence*, éd. L'Harmattan, 1997
- Hazan, Katy, *Les Orphelins de la Shoah , Les Maisons de l'Espoir (1944 – 1960)*, éd. Les Belles Lettres, 2000
- Jablonka, Ivan, *Histoire des Grands-Parents que je n'ai pas eus*, éd. du Seuil, 2012
- Muller, Annette, *La Petite fille du Veld'Hiv*, éd. Centre de recherche et de documentation sur les camps d'internement et la déportation juive dans le Loiret (CERCIL), Orléans, 2009
- Popiolek, Claude, *La Douce France, ce Jour-là*, éd. Amalthée, 2014
- Schwarz, Lotte, *Je veux Vivre jusqu'à ma Mort*, éd. du Seuil, 1979

Books in German:
- Martens, Dr. Holger, *Auf dem Weg in den Widerstand: Die "Echo"-Versammlung der Hamburger SPD 1933*, Arbeitsgemeinschaft verfolgter Sozialdemokraten, Hamburg 2010
- Meitmann, Jack, *Konsequente Demokratie*, Frieling Verlag, Berlin 1992

Index

A

Adam, Hans · 36, 121, 140
Adam, Hermann ("*Opa Adam*") · 17, 21, 119, 132, 138, 139, 142, 153
Adam-Grotkopp, Emma ("*Emmi*") · 129, 140, 142
Adam-Meitmann, Else ("*Mutti*") · 16, 21, 22, 25, 26, 28, 31, 36, 37, 38, 41, 45, 66, 72, 73, 75, 76, 79, 87, 89, 95, 97, 106, 109, 113, 115, 116, 117, 119, 121, 122, 125, 134, 137, 139, 140, 141, 142, 143, 144, 146, 147, 148, 153, 159, 160, 161, 162, 185, 186
Adam-Schultze, Anni · 21, 140
Ainay-le-Château · 207
Aix-les-Bains · 65
Allier · 207
Al-Malik-Saud-Al-Awal · 133
Alps · 65, 175, 184
Alsace · 186
Altona · 19, 157
America · 163
Amsterdam · 48
Andersen, Dr Hermann · 39
Andrésy · 65, 68, 69, 77, 79, 85, 97
Angoulême · 204
Anklam · 150
Annenstrasse, Kiel, Gaarden · 137
Annette · 240
Antaeus · 92
Apt · 188
Argence · 115
Armenia · 214
Atlantic · 68, 210
Auschwitz · 49, 54, 118, 175, 177, 198, 201, 208
Austerlitz Station, Paris · 207
Auvergne · 59
Auvers-sur-Oise · 88
Auxy · 199
Axel · 29

B

Bachstrasse, Jena · 43
Bagneux, Cemetery · 203, 213
Baltic Sea · 30, 145, 166
Bargue, *Rue*, Paris · 56, 58, 65, 68, 72, 173, 201, 210, 213
BASF · 178
Bäsler · 143
Bayer · 178
Beaune-la-Rolande · 175, 198, 231, 232
Beauregard, Villa, Nice · 59
Beauvais · 57
Belgium · 53
Bergen-Belsen · 180
Berlin · 28, 35, 36, 37, 38, 39, 41, 42, 45, 66, 67, 91, 116, 140, 141, 143, 194, 235, 236, 238, 240
Berton · 203
Bessarabia · 214
Betty · 75
Birkenau, Auschwitz II · 177
Blumes-Popiolek, Cecilia · 198
Boelcke-Kaserne, Nordhausen · 180
Bonn · 115, 122, 144
Bonnieux · 187, 188
Bourget, Le · 181, 183

241

Brandenburg Gate · 36
Brecht, Bertolt · 141
Bremerhaven · 51
British Columbia · 167
Brodersen, Anne and Niels · 36
Bruges · 48
Brunner, Alois · 176
Brym, Micha · 62, 63, 95, 237
Brym-Desarthe, Esther · 62, 63, 237
Buchenwald · 55, 165
Buna · 177
Bundestag · 88, 158
Bürgerschaft · 20, 46, 156
Burgundy · 72, 198
Busch, Ernst · 141, 159

C

California · 151, 167
Campbell, Ainslie · 238
Canada · 167
CCE · 59, 60, 63, 64, 73, 77, 80, 86, 87, 89, 93, 97, 186, 237
Champs-Élysées · 82
Channel, English · 109

Chaponval · 88
Charente · 204
Charité, Hospital · 41, 235, 236, 238
Charlottenburg · 35
Charonne, *Rue de*, Paris · 122
Cher · 207
Chezal-Benoît · 207
Chleuhs · 189
Civray · 204, 205, 208
Clinic of Metal Industry Workers, Paris · 94
Cochem · 122
Cohen-Reuss, Max · 66
Colonel-Fabien, Avenue, Livry-Gargan · 85, 94
Concentration Camp · 11, 25, 60, 95
Concentration camps · 118
consumer cooperative · 17, 132, 140
Cooper, Fenimore · 153
Copenhagen · 166
Cosnefroy-Bruzeau-Popiolek, Marguerite ("*Tante Margot*") · 198

Coteaux, Avenue des, Le Raincy · 77, 93, 102

D

Dabrowski, Marcel · 199
Daix · 112
Dakota · 182
Daquin, Louis · 83
De Dietrich · 186
De Gaulle, Charles, General · 90
Demarcation Line · 198, 199, 208
Denmark · 166
Denouval, Manoir, Andrésy · 65, 74, 75
Deportation-Transport
#05 of 06/28/1942 · 199
#09 of 07/22/1942 · 198
#13 of 07/31/1942 · 201
#16 of 08/06/1942 · 201
#42 of 11/06/1942 · 205
#45 of 11/11/1942 · 198

#73 of 05/15/1944 · 198
#76 of 06/30/1944 · 177
Dijon · 198
Dittmer, Wilhelm · 50
Djiki · 73
Dora, Nordhausen · 179, 180, 181
Drancy · 175, 176, 177, 181, 198, 205, 225, 226, 227, 230, 231
Drossen · 26, 30, 32
Duclos, Jacques · 90
Dupetit-Thouars, Cité, Paris · 195

E

Eisler, Hanns · 141
Ellerbeck · 153, 158
Ellis Island · 166, 216
England · 49
Estonia · 198
Europe · 50, 200

F

Favorites, Rue des, Paris · 176
Feist-Adam, Anna ("Oma") · 21, 22, 25, 26, 28, 36, 37, 39, 76, 83, 119, 121, 129, 138, 143, 144
Ferguson, John · 216
Flensburg · 155
Fontenay-aux-Roses · 81, 186
Forge, La, Children's home · 81
France · 40, 49, 53, 54, 72, 75, 83, 84, 90, 91, 106, 120, 193, 200, 220, 240
Francès, Robert · 179, 240
Frankfurt/Oder · 26, 28
French Communist Party · 90
Freud, Sigmund · 177
Freyming · 203
Friedrich-Wilhelm-Universität · 41
Friends of Wlocławek Society · 194
Fuhlsbüttel · 19, 25, 45, 157

G

Gaarden · 132, 137, 139, 149, 151, 158
Gaarden cooperative Bakery · 153
Gaea · 92
Gardelegen · 180
Gardner, Joyce · 238
Gayk, Andreas und Frieda · 35, 36
GEG · 132, 154
Geneanet · 217
Geneva · 89
German Occupation · 208
German Revolution · 142
Germany · 46, 49, 88, 92, 115, 144, 158, 171, 194, 199
Gerszanowicz-Popiolek, Soura Riwka ("Sonia") · 205
Gestapo · 25, 26, 40, 157
Gleiwitz · 179
Glogau · 30, 138
Goldfarb, Felicitas ("Fée") · 79, 82, 86
Goldman, Franck · 211, 212, 213, 214
Goldman, Lewis (Louis) · 211, 212, 213, 214, 215
Goldman-Chant, Dorothy (Dora) · 211, 212
Goldman-Klein, Ellen · 215

Göring · 42
Granville · 109
Great-Britain · 40, 165, 168
Greifswald · 151
Grotkopp, Wilhelm ("*Willi*") · 129
Grumbach, Salomon · 52
Gülck, Carl, "*Karlemann*" · 167
Gülck, Hans · 151, 167

H

Hallerstrasse, Hamburg · 45, 47
Hamburg · 10, 13, 19, 25, 26, 28, 37, 45, 53, 54, 63, 65, 72, 75, 82, 83, 88, 91, 119, 120, 132, 133, 143, 144, 148, 151, 154, 157, 186, 240
Hamburg University · 132
Hamburg-America-Line · 209, 214
Hardy, Oliver · 138
Harmsstrasse, Kiel · 144
Hasseldieksdamm · 17
Havel · 141
Heiligenhafen · 148

Hélène · 102, 111, 113, 117, 122, 237
Hellig Olaf, ship · 166
Hermberg · 42
Heydorn, Heinz-Joachim · 50
Heymannstrasse, Hamburg · 47, 120
Himmler · 178
Hindenburg · 25
Hitler · 25, 40, 45, 123, 143, 157, 200
Höchst · 178
Holocaust · 53, 57
Holstenstrasse, Kiel · 144
Horn, Modehaus, Hamburg · 46
Humanité, L', newspaper · 90

I

Iena · 132, 143
IG Farbenindustrie · 178
Independent Labour Party · 50
International School, Geneva · 89
Internet · 163, 165, 210, 211
Israel · 211
Issoudun · 199, 208

Italy · 106

J

Jablonski, Ernst ("*Jouhi*") · 81
Jabouille, Raymonde · 199, 206, 208, 237
Jacqueline · 94
Jardins Saint-Paul, *Rue*, Paris · 172
Jena · 42, 43
Joint · 64, 77

K

Kaiser · 142
Kapp-Putsch · 155
Kathrin II, czarina · 139
Kharkov/Kharkiv ("*Karkoff*") · 172, 196
Kiel · 15, 16, 17, 21, 25, 28, 29, 36, 37, 38, 39, 40, 45, 83, 121, 123, 131, 137, 139, 140, 141, 142, 143, 144, 147, 148, 149, 150, 156, 157, 158, 163, 164, 166, 168
Kiel City Hospital · 161

Kieler Strasse
(Gaarden) · 149
Kiel-Falckenstein ·
147
Klein, Adolf ("*Onkel
Adolf*") · 151
Klein-Meitmann,
Louise · 150,
151
Klingbeil, Anna
Katharina · 42
Klosterfelde · 143
Knesebeckstrasse,
Berlin · 35, 38,
42
Kolafu · 25
Köster, Dr Adolf ·
155
Krakowska-Sciarke,
Adèle · 194
Kurfürstendamm,
Berlin · 42

L

Laboe · 30, 141
Leslau · 191
Lévy-Valensi, Prof. ·
207, 208
Lipsheim · 186
Lithuania · 198
Livry-Gargan · 85,
87, 91, 93, 94,
97, 111
London · 50, 51, 52,
73, 75, 77, 198
London, Jack · 153
Lorraine · 203, 204
Los Angeles · 151,
167

Louvre, Museum,
Paris · 106
Lower Silesia · 30
Lübeck · 39, 133,
147
Luftwaffe · 204
Lunet, Zette and
Pierre · 66, 69,
77, 90, 93, 102,
237
Lutétia, Hotel, Paris
· 183
Lynn Valley,
Vancouver · 167
Lyons · 198

M

Madeleine · 87, 95
Magali · 10, 51,
122, 123, 125,
126, 146, 147,
185, 187, 188
Maienweg,
Hamburg-
Fuhlsbüttel · 20
Mandschurei · 26
Mans, Le · 51, 52,
53, 184, 185,
186
Marceau, Marcel ·
186
Marne · 113
Massif Central · 59
Maurette, Marie-
Thérèse · 89
May Events, 1968 ·
187
May, Karl · 153
McCarthyism · 77

Mecklenburg · 151,
152
Mediterranean Sea
· 59, 61, 65
Méhoncourt, Castle
· 53, 184
Mehr Demokratie,
Society · 134
Meitmann, Anton ·
151, 163, 164,
165, 166, 168,
169
Meitmann, Gabriel ·
150
Meitmann, Hans ·
152
Meitmann, Heinrich
("*Hein*",
"*Heiner*") · 164,
166, 167, 169
Meitmann, Heinrich
Jr I · 168
Meitmann, Heinrich
Jr II ("*Henry*",
"*Hank*") · 168
Meitmann, Jack
("*Jacki*") · 12, 15,
17, 20, 21, 22,
23, 26, 29, 36,
37, 38, 41, 98,
99, 106, 109,
112, 121, 124,
129, 131, 133,
134, 140, 143,
145, 147, 148,
162, 163, 164,
165, 168, 186
Meitmann,
Johannes I Jr. ·
168, 169

Meitmann, Johannes Sr. · 17, 149, 150, 153
Meitmann, Karl ("*Vati*", "*Opa*") · 16, 19, 25, 26, 27, 28, 29, 32, 35, 36, 38, 40, 41, 45, 46, 66, 73, 83, 87, 89, 91, 106, 109, 115, 119, 121, 132, 134, 141, 142, 144, 145, 147, 149, 151, 152, 157, 158, 161, 162, 163, 166
Meitmann, Wilhelm ("*Bill*") · 151, 163, 164, 166
Meitmann, Wilhelm ("*Willimann*") · 165
Meitmann-Cooper-Mastin, Carmen · 165, 168, 238
Meitmann-Gülck, Elsa ("*Else*") · 151, 167
Meitmann-Hansen, Luisa ("*Lissi*") · 151
Meitmann-Poschar, Wilhelmine ("*Minna*") · 151
Meitmann-Stermann, Grete ("*Grète*") · 9, 10, 11, 12, 15, 18, 21, 28, 29, 30, 35, 36, 37, 38, 50, 54, 60, 61, 62, 82, 87, 101, 102, 103, 105, 117, 125, 126, 127, 131, 133, 143, 147, 148, 149, 152, 158, 162, 165, 168, 171, 186, 188, 217, 234, 235, 236
Meldeamt, Kiel · 165
Merlebach · 203, 204, 205, 206
Metz · 204
Meyer, Gerold · 51
Meyer-Abel-Meitmann, Johanne · 151, 152
Mickey · 64
Mittelbau · 180
Moldavia · 214
Monge, *Rue*, Paris · 54
Mongolei · 26
Mönkeberg · 123, 124, 134, 143, 144, 145, 147, 158, 159
Monowitz, Auschwitz III · 177
Montfermeil · 115, 116, 118, 119
Morvan · 72
Moselle · 122
Movement for Peace · 90, 111
MRAP, Anti-Racist Movement · 72
Müritz Lake · 37, 141
Muschi · 64, 73

N

Naïe Presse, newspaper · 173
National-Socialist · 31
Nazi · 60
New-York · 166
Nice · 59, 60, 62, 63, 64, 65, 71, 77, 95, 233, 234
Niendorf · 26
Nimptsch · 139
Nivillers · 57, 61
Nord-Express · 53
Nordhausen · 179, 181
Normandy · 115, 198
North Sea · 51, 91
North train station, Paris · 53, 92
North-Schleswig, plebiscite · 155
Norway · 75

O

Occupied Zone · 205
Odessa · 197

Oise · 88
Ontario, CA, USA · 167
Opel · 134
Oranienburg · 45, 143
Orléans · 175, 198, 201, 240
OSE, Children Aid Organization · 53, 55, 184

P

Pacific, Ocean · 168
Pain, appliances · 186
Pankow-Meitmann, Anna ("*Anni*") · 168
Panthéon, Paris · 54
Paris · 53, 57, 65, 66, 75, 194, 197, 206, 212, 221
Passat, sailing boat · 161
Pavillons-sous-Bois, Les · 94
Peene · 150
Pessicart, Avenue, Nice · 59
Pétain, Philippe, Field Marshall · 175, 183
Peter III, Czar · 139
Philadelphia · 209, 210, 211, 212, 213, 214
Picardy · 59
Pif · 88

Pithiviers · 175, 201, 229, 230
Plateau, *Allée du*, Le Raincy · 77, 79, 82, 86, 93, 94, 102
Plattdüütsch · 166
Poissy · 75
Poitiers · 205, 206, 207
Poland · 118, 138, 171, 172, 193, 214
Polkwitz · 30
Pomerania · 150, 152
Popilok, David · 193
Popiolek, Abram ("*Avrum*", "*Albert*") · 192, 193, 203, 205, 208, 232, 237
Popiolek, Alexander ("*Sender*", "*Alexandre*") · 95, 184, 192, 198
Popiolek, Beer ("*Bejek*") · 192, 193, 197
Popiolek, Claude · 238, 240
Popiolek, Hersz ("*Henri*") · 192, 193, 197, 198, 230
Popiolek, Jakob ("*Yankel*", "*Jacques*") · 192, 193, 198, 199, 231

Popiolek, Nachman · 192, 193, 198, 231, 237
Popiolek, Nussen ("*Nathan*") · 192, 193, 198, 199, 206, 237
Popiolek, Victor · 205, 206
Popiolek, Wolf · 191, 193
Popiolek-Popilok, Mojsze Icek (Maurice) · 191, 193, 197
Popiolek-Stermann, Rojzla ("*Rachel*") · 172, 191, 192, 193, 194, 196, 197, 200, 213, 230
Poplar Street, Philadelphia · 200, 210, 211
Popolick · 206
Prague · 157
Preetz · 134, 168
Provence · 10, 122
Putigneux, Impasse, Paris · 195
Putschlau · 30, 138

R

Raincy, Le · 9, 77, 79, 82, 83, 93, 103, 105, 106, 109, 113, 118, 122
Rathenaupark · 19

247

Red Army · 178
Red Cross · 85, 148
Red-Cross · 211
Reichsbanner · 19, 156
Reichstag · 25
Ribnitz · 151
Riviera · 59
Rockefeller · 216
Röhrdanz · 42
Rollin, *Rue*, Paris · 53, 54, 55, 102, 104, 105, 117
Romania · 186
Romatzki · 42
Rose · 86, 89, 91
Rosette · 102, 237
Rostock · 151, 152
Rothschild Hospital, Paris · 171
Rousseau, Jean-Jacques · 160
Routier · 175, 176
Rozenholc-Popiolek, Szprynça ("*Solange*") · 184, 186
Rusheweyh, Dr Herbert · 158
Russia · 172

S

Sainte-Anne, Hospital, Paris · 203, 207, 208
Sainte-Maxime · 61
Saint-Florent-sur-Cher · 199
Saint-Germain-des-Prés, Paris · 183
Saints-Pères, Hôtel des, Paris · 183
Saint-Tropez · 61
Salpétrière-Hospital, Paris · 207
Savoy · 65
Schakowsky-Meitmann, Amalie ("*Male*", "*Mali*") · 165
Schlakar-Goldman, Nachman-Meyer (Myer) · 211, 214, 215
Schleswig · 154, 158
Schleswig-Holstein · 16, 19, 152, 154, 155, 156
Schmagorei · 26, 27, 28, 29, 30, 33
Schöneiche · 36
Schulimowitz, Itzig · 215
Schwarz, Lotte · 53, 54, 55, 56, 66, 69, 76, 81, 89, 101, 102, 104, 105, 115, 117, 122, 184, 185, 187, 240
Schwarz-Languepin, Anna Judith ("*Anjuta*", "*Aniou*") · 76, 101, 106, 185, 187

Schwedterstrasse, Berlin · 42
Scotland · 51
Seattle · 168, 169
Segal, Gilles · 186
Seine · 66, 88, 207
Settons · 72
Shoah Memorial, Paris · 195
Siarka-Popiolek, Ruchla · 192, 193, 194
Siarka-Sciarke, Alexander (Alexandre, "*Sender*") · 194
Siemsen, Anna · 49
Silesia · 138
Singer · 105
Smyrek, Modehaus, Jena · 42
Soldan, sceneries · 143
SPD · 19, 20, 45, 46, 66, 89, 132, 134, 139, 156, 157, 240
SS · 26, 40, 176, 178, 180, 181
Stadtkloster, Kiel · 144
Stalingrad · 62
Stary Rynek · 192
Stermann, Camille · 54, 56, 71, 91, 171, 173, 175, 176, 177, 179, 180, 181, 195, 213, 215, 225
Stermann, Catherine

("Catia") · 10, 11, 73, 75, 76, 77, 81, 82, 83, 86, 87, 88, 91, 92, 95, 96, 101, 102, 103, 105, 106, 109, 110, 111, 113, 114, 115, 116, 117, 120, 121, 122, 124, 125, 126, 127, 133, 137, 143, 159, 172, 173
Stermann, David · 68, 106, 173, 175, 184, 199, 203, 238
Stermann, Gilles · 10, 11, 124, 159
Stermann, Henry ("Rémy") · 10, 13, 49, 51, 52, 53, 54, 55, 56, 57, 59, 60, 61, 63, 66, 67, 68, 69, 73, 75, 76, 77, 79, 80, 83, 87, 88, 89, 90, 91, 92, 93, 94, 95, 96, 97, 98, 102, 103, 104, 105, 109, 111, 112, 115, 116, 117, 119, 122, 125, 130, 146, 161, 162, 171, 172, 173, 174, 175, 176, 178, 180, 181, 183, 184, 185, 186, 191, 201, 203, 210, 213, 215, 225
Stermann, Michel ("Micha") · 9, 62, 95, 96, 105, 120, 122, 123, 124, 133, 141
Stermann, Nathan · 173, 174, 175, 176, 180, 226
Stermann-Wolf, Monique · 68, 173, 175, 184
Stettin · 139
Stockholm · 48
Stralsund · 150
Strasburg · 186
Stravinsky, Igor · 158
Sütterlin · 23
Switzerland · 49, 51, 52, 65, 109
Sylt · 91
Syria · 176
Szulamowicz?-Goldman, Esther · 200, 210, 211, 213, 214
Szulamowicz?-Stermann Lajzer (Leiser, "Lazare") · 172, 193, 194, 195, 196, 200, 213, 228, 229

T

Table Ronde, La · 57
Tarnos · 68
Tello · 29
Thälmann, Ernst · 165
Theaterkunst · 42

U

UJRE · 59, 99, 186
UNESCO · 89
USA · 62, 200, 209
US-Army · 180
Usedom · 150
USSR · 94

V

V2 · 180
Van Gogh · 88
Vancouver · 151, 167, 168
Varoqueaux · 96
Vel d'Hiv, velodrome · 90, 175, 201
Vélo-Solex · 104
Vernon, BC, Canada · 167
Vichy Regime · 200
Vienna · 179
Vienne · 204
Vigée-Lebrun, Rue, Paris · 175
Villa, Pancho · 164

Violet, *Rue*, Paris · 184
Vistula · 191
Volkswagen · 106, 109, 158
Volvo · 161

W

Wansleben · 181
Warsaw · 197, 214, 215
Wartburgstrasse, Jena · 42

Washington · 168
Wehrmacht · 40, 204
West-Sternberg · 26
Wichené, Simon · 52
Wikipedia · 127
Włocławek · 191, 194, 197, 199, 213, 214, 215
Wolgast · 150, 151, 168
World War I · 16
World-Wide Web · 166, 210, 217

Y

Yad Vashem · 176

Z

Żabia, *Ulica*, Włocławek · 191
Zielenzig · 26
Zurich · 49

Table of contents

PREFACE TO THE READER OF THE ENGLISH EDITION 7
TO MAMAN GRÈTE 9

YOUR STORY 15

YOUR START IN LIFE 15
FAREWELL FROM KIEL 19
BANISHED 25
BACK TO A BIG CITY 35
WAR 37
PSYCHIC CRISIS AND THEN SEAMSTRESS APPRENTICESHIP 41
PEACE 45
RÉMY 49
EMIGRANT 53
REJECTED 55
UJRE-CCE, NICE 59
ANDRÉSY 65
PREGNANCY 71
CATIA 75
LE RAINCY (1) 79
LIVRY-GARGAN 85
LE RAINCY (2) 93
RESIGNING FROM THE UJRE-CCE 97
CRACKED VERTEBRA 101
BACK TO NORMAL LIFE 109
THE END 115
EPILOGUE 117
WORDPLAYS 129

PORTRAITS OF MATERNAL RELATIVES 131

JACKI 131
MUTTI 137
OPA 149
ADVENTURE OF THE THREE MEITMANN BROTHERS 163

PORTRAITS OF PATERNAL RELATIVES 171

Rémy	171
Lajzer and Rojzla	191
Rich marriage in Merlebach or Should one believe in family legends?	203
444 Poplar Street	209
Conclusion	217

DOCUMENTS 219

Thanks	237
Bibliography	239
Index	241
Table of contents	251